CONTENTS

The Low-Carb Lowdown   2

Blazing Beef   4

Patio-Perfect Pork   24

Pleasing Poultry   40

Sizzling Seafood   60

Smoking Sides   84

Index   95

THE LOW-CARB LOWDOWN

INFORMATION ABOUT THE LOW-CARB RECIPES IN THIS BOOK.

Weight loss fads come and go, but it certainly seems that counting carbohydrates will be an important part of many lives for the foreseeable future. With that in mind, the recipes in this book were selected for people following a variety of low-carb eating plans. No matter which diet you're on, or what phase of that plan you're in, from induction to maintenance, you will find delicious low-carb options. Other nutritional data, including calorie count and fat content for each recipe, are also included to provide the information you need to make smart nutritional choices.

HOW LOW IS LOW?

The recipes in this book all contain less than 15 net grams of carbohydrate per serving. Net grams are defined as total grams of carbohydrate minus grams of fiber. In other words, if a serving contains 18 grams of carbohydrate with 5 grams of fiber, it would have 13 net grams of carbohydrate and would fall within these guidelines. The total carb count and the fiber count are provided for each recipe so you can calculate net grams yourself.

Nutrients per serving: 98 Calories, 18g Carbohydrate,
5g Dietary Fiber, 2g Total Fat, <1g Saturated Fat
0 mg Cholesterol, 92mg Sodium, 3g Protein

**18g carbs
–5g fiber**

13g net carbs

LOW-CARB SWEETENERS

Some recipes in this book use small amounts of regular sugar instead of, or in addition to, sugar substitute. In these cases, the addition of sugar improved the flavor or texture enough to be worth raising the carbohydrate count. You can, of course, use the sugar substitute of your choice, if you prefer. In recipes for baked goods, however, substitutions can affect the texture of the final dish, in addition to its flavor. The generic description of the brand of sugar substitute used is indicated where it might be important to the success of the recipe based on our testing.

NUTRITIONAL NUMBERS

The nutritional information provided with each recipe is intended only to help you plan a healthy diet. The numbers are approximate and intended to be guidelines only. Garnishes, serving suggestions and optional ingredients are NOT included in the calculations. Where a range of amounts or a choice of ingredients is shown in the ingredients list (i.e., 4 to 5 cups broth or wine) nutritional calculations are based on the smaller amount (4 cups) and the first ingredient shown (broth). Items included in the photo but not listed in the recipe ingredient list are NOT included in the calculations. Since the numbers are based on individual servings, it's important to take portion size into consideration to get an accurate nutritional picture.

Sticking to a healthy diet long term is considerably easier when you are enjoying great-tasting, easy-to-fix meals. The recipes in this book can make even the restrictive phases of a low-carb program very easy to swallow.

BLAZING BEEF

Peppered Steak with Dijon Sauce

4 boneless beef top loin (New York strip) steaks, cut 1 inch thick
  (about 1½ pounds)
1 tablespoon *French's*® Worcestershire Sauce
  Crushed black pepper
⅓ cup mayonnaise
⅓ cup *French's*® Honey Dijon Mustard
3 tablespoons dry red wine
2 tablespoons minced red or green onion
2 tablespoons minced fresh parsley
1 clove garlic, minced

1. Brush steaks with Worcestershire and sprinkle with pepper to taste; set aside. To prepare Dijon sauce, combine mayonnaise, mustard, wine, onion, parsley and garlic in medium bowl.

2. Place steaks on grid. Grill steaks over high heat 15 minutes for medium rare or to desired doneness, turning often. Serve with Dijon sauce. Garnish as desired. *Makes 4 servings*

Tip: Dijon sauce is also great served with grilled salmon and swordfish. To serve with fish, substitute white wine for red wine and minced dill for fresh parsley.

Prep Time: 10 minutes
Cook Time: 15 minutes

Nutrients per Serving (¼ total recipe): 416 Calories, 2g Carbohydrate, <1g Dietary Fiber, 25g Total Fat, 6g Saturated Fat, 107mg Cholesterol, 697mg Sodium, 37g Protein

Peppered Steak with Dijon Sauce

Grilled Beef Salad

½ cup mayonnaise
2 tablespoons cider vinegar or white wine vinegar
1 tablespoon spicy brown mustard
2 cloves garlic, minced
½ teaspoon sugar
6 cups torn assorted lettuces such as romaine, red leaf and Bibb
1 large tomato, seeded and chopped
⅓ cup chopped fresh basil
2 slices red onion, separated into rings
1 boneless beef top sirloin steak (about 1 pound)
½ teaspoon salt
½ teaspoon black pepper
½ cup herb or garlic croutons
Additional black pepper (optional)

1. Prepare grill for direct cooking. Combine mayonnaise, vinegar, mustard, garlic and sugar in small bowl; mix well. Cover; refrigerate until ready to serve.

2. Toss together lettuce, tomato, basil and onion in large bowl. Cover; refrigerate until ready to serve.

3. Sprinkle both sides of steak with salt and black pepper. Place steak on grid. Grill, uncovered, over medium heat 13 to 16 minutes for medium-rare to medium or until desired doneness, turning once.

4. Transfer steak to cutting board. Slice in half lengthwise; carve crosswise into thin slices.

5. Add steak and croutons to bowl with lettuce mixture; toss well. Add mayonnaise mixture; toss until well coated. Serve with additional black pepper, if desired.   *Makes 4 servings*

Nutrients per Serving (¼ of total recipe): 405 Calories, 11g Carbohydrate, 3g Dietary Fiber, 28g Total Fat, 5g Saturated Fat, 80mg Cholesterol, 634mg Sodium, 27g Protein

Grilled Beef Salad

The Definitive Steak

4 boneless beef top loin (strip) steaks, cut 1 inch thick (about
    5 ounces each)
¼ cup olive oil
2 teaspoons minced garlic
1 teaspoon salt
½ teaspoon black pepper

1. Place steaks in shallow glass container. Combine oil, garlic, salt and pepper in small bowl; mix well. Pour oil mixture over steaks; turn to coat well. Cover; refrigerate 30 to 60 minutes.

2. Prepare grill for direct cooking.

3. Place steaks on grid. Grill, covered, over medium-high heat 14 minutes for medium, 20 minutes for well or until desired doneness, turning halfway through grilling time. *Makes 4 servings*

Nutrients per Serving (¼ of total recipe): 438 Calories, 1g Carbohydrate, <1g Dietary Fiber, 35g Total Fat, 10g Saturated Fat, 74mg Cholesterol, 654mg Sodium, 29g Protein

Peppercorn Steaks

2 tablespoons olive oil
1 to 2 teaspoons cracked red or black peppercorns or freshly ground
    pepper
1 teaspoon minced garlic
1 teaspoon dried herbs, such as rosemary or parsley
4 boneless beef top loin (strip) or ribeye steaks (6 ounces each)
¼ teaspoon salt

1. Combine oil, peppercorns, garlic and herbs in small bowl. Rub mixture on both sides of each steak. Cover; refrigerate 30 to 60 minutes.

2. Prepare grill for direct cooking.

3. Place steaks on grid over medium heat. Grill, uncovered, 10 to 12 minutes for medium-rare to medium or until desired doneness, turning occasionally. Season with salt after cooking. *Makes 4 servings*

Nutrients per Serving (¼ of total recipe): 413 Calories, <1g Carbohydrate, <1g Dietary Fiber, 23g Total Fat, 7g Saturated Fat, 129mg Cholesterol, 249mg Sodium, 49g Protein

Honey Mustard Steaks with Grilled Onions

4 boneless beef top loin (strip) steaks, cut 1 inch thick
$\frac{1}{3}$ cup coarse-grain Dijon-style mustard
1 tablespoon plus 1$\frac{1}{2}$ teaspoons honey
1 tablespoon chopped parsley
1 tablespoon cider vinegar
1 tablespoon water
$\frac{1}{4}$ teaspoon hot pepper sauce
$\frac{1}{8}$ teaspoon coarsely ground black pepper
1 large red onion, sliced $\frac{1}{2}$ inch thick

Combine mustard, honey, parsley, vinegar, water, hot pepper sauce and pepper. Place beef steaks and onion slices on grid over medium coals; brush both with mustard mixture. Grill 9 to 12 minutes for rare (140°F) to medium (160°F), turning once and brushing with mustard mixture.

Makes 4 servings

Prep Time: 30 minutes

Favorite recipe from **North Dakota Beef Commission**

Nutrients per Serving ($\frac{1}{4}$ of total recipe): 221 Calories, 9g Carbohydrate, 1g Dietary Fiber, 7g Total Fat, 3g Saturated Fat, 66mg Cholesterol, 520mg Sodium, 25g Protein

Hot Tip

Beef provides high-quality protein, including all eight essential amino acids; it is also an important source of dietary iron and zinc. Today, over 40% of beef cuts have no external fat at all. So if you are trying to choose lean cuts of beef, look for "loin" or "round" in the name, such as sirloin, tenderloin or top round—these are the leanest.

Guadalajara Beef and Salsa

1 bottle (12 ounces) Mexican dark beer*
¼ cup soy sauce
2 cloves garlic, minced
1 teaspoon *each* ground cumin, chili powder and hot pepper sauce
4 boneless beef sirloin or top loin strip steaks (4 to 6 ounces each)
   Salt and black pepper
   Red, green and yellow bell peppers, cut lengthwise into quarters, seeded (optional)
   Salsa (recipe follows)
   Lime wedges

*Substitute any beer for Mexican dark beer.

Combine beer, soy sauce, garlic, cumin, chili powder and hot pepper sauce in large shallow glass dish or large heavy plastic food storage bag. Add beef; cover dish or close bag. Marinate in refrigerator up to 12 hours, turning beef several times. Remove beef from marinade; discard marinade. Season with salt and black pepper.

Oil hot grid to help prevent sticking. Grill beef and bell peppers, if desired, on covered grill, over medium KINGSFORD® Briquets, 8 to 12 minutes, turning once, or until beef reaches medium doneness and peppers are tender. Serve with salsa and lime wedges. *Makes 4 servings*

Nutrients per Serving (¼ of total recipe without bell peppers or Salsa): 209 Calories, 6g Carbohydrate, 1g Dietary Fiber, 9g Total Fat, 2g Saturated Fat, 69mg Cholesterol, 457mg Sodium, 25g Protein

Salsa

2 cups coarsely chopped seeded tomatoes
2 green onions with tops, sliced
1 clove garlic, minced
1 to 2 teaspoons minced seeded jalapeño or serrano chili pepper*
1 tablespoon olive or vegetable oil
2 to 3 teaspoons lime juice
8 to 10 sprigs fresh cilantro, minced (optional)
½ teaspoon salt or to taste
½ teaspoon sugar or to taste
¼ teaspoon black pepper

*Jalapeño peppers can sting and irritate the skin; wear rubber gloves when handling peppers and do not touch eyes. Wash hands after handling.

continued on page 12

Guadalajara Beef and Salsa

Guadalajara Beef and Salsa, continued

Combine tomatoes, green onions, garlic, chili pepper, oil and lime juice in medium bowl. Stir in cilantro, if desired. Season with salt, sugar and black pepper. Adjust seasonings to taste, adding additional lime juice or chili pepper, if desired.   *Makes about 2 cups*

Nutrients per Serving (2 tablespoons): 13 Calories, 1g Carbohydrate, <1g Dietary Fiber, 1g Total Fat, <1g Saturated Fat, 0mg Cholesterol, 74mg Sodium, <1g Protein

Korean Beef Short Ribs

2½ **pounds beef chuck flanken-style short ribs, cut ⅜ to ½ inch thick***
¼ **cup chopped green onions**
¼ **cup water**
¼ **cup soy sauce**
1 **tablespoon sugar**
2 **teaspoons grated fresh ginger**
2 **teaspoons dark sesame oil**
2 **cloves garlic, minced**
½ **teaspoon black pepper**
1 **tablespoon sesame seeds, toasted**

*Flanken-style ribs can be ordered from your butcher. They are cross-cut short ribs sawed through the bones.

1. Place ribs in large resealable plastic food storage bag. Combine green onions, water, soy sauce, sugar, ginger, oil, garlic and pepper in small bowl; pour over ribs. Seal bag tightly; turn to coat. Marinate in refrigerator at least 4 hours or up to 24 hours, turning occasionally.

2. Prepare grill for direct cooking.

3. Drain ribs; reserve marinade. Place ribs on grid. Grill ribs, covered, over medium-hot coals 5 minutes. Brush tops lightly with reserved marinade; turn and brush again. Discard remaining marinade. Continue to grill, covered, 5 to 6 minutes for medium or until desired doneness. Sprinkle with sesame seeds.   *Makes 4 to 6 servings*

Nutrients per Serving (¼ of total recipe): 416 Calories, 6g Carbohydrate, 1g Dietary Fiber, 23g Total Fat, 9g Saturated Fat, 124mg Cholesterol, 1153mg Sodium, 42g Protein

Herbed Beef Kabobs

> 1 cup LAWRY'S® Herb & Garlic Marinade With Lemon Juice, divided
> 1 to 1½ pounds boneless, beef top sirloin, cut into chunks
> 12 mushrooms
> 2 medium green bell peppers, cut into 1½-inch squares
> 2 medium onions, cut into chunks
> Skewers

In large resealable plastic bag, combine ¾ cup Herb & Garlic Marinade and beef. Seal bag and marinate in refrigerator for 30 minutes, turning several times. Remove beef from bag, discarding used marinade. On skewers, alternate beef with vegetables until all are used. Grill or broil to desired degree of doneness, about 10 to 14 minutes, brushing with remaining ¼ cup Marinade. *Makes 4 to 6 servings*

Hint: Soak wooden skewers in water for at least 15 minutes to help prevent burning.

Prep Time: 15 minutes
Marinate Time: 30 minutes
Cook Time: 10 to 14 minutes

Nutrients per Serving (⅙ of total recipe): 191 Calories, 8g Carbohydrate, 2g Dietary Fiber, 5g Total Fat, 2g Saturated Fat, 69mg Cholesterol, 354mg Sodium, 26g Protein

Grilled Steak

> 4 boneless sirloin or ribeye steaks (about 5 ounces each)
> CARB OPTIONS™ Steak Sauce

Season steak, if desired, with salt and ground black pepper. Grill or broil until desired doneness. Serve with Carb Options Steak Sauce. *Makes 4 servings*

Preparation Time: 5 minutes
Cook Time: 12 minutes

Nutrients per Serving (1 Grilled Steak): 150 Calories, 1g Carbohydrate, 0g Dietary Fiber, 5g Total Fat, 2g Saturated Fat, 70mg Cholesterol, 250mg Sodium, 23g Protein

Herbed Beef Kabobs

Steak Provençal

  4 beef sirloin, tenderloin or ribeye steaks (about 11 ounces each)
  5 tablespoons I CAN'T BELIEVE IT'S NOT BUTTER!® Spread
  2 large cloves garlic, finely chopped
1½ cups chopped tomatoes (about 2 medium)
  1 to 2 tablespoons rinsed and chopped large capers
 ¼ teaspoon salt
 ¼ teaspoon ground black pepper
  2 tablespoons chopped fresh parsley

Grill or broil steaks to desired doneness.

Meanwhile, in 10-inch skillet, melt I Can't Believe It's Not Butter!® Spread and cook garlic over medium heat, stirring occasionally, 30 seconds. Add tomatoes, capers, salt and pepper. Cook, stirring occasionally, 3 minutes or until tomatoes are cooked and mixture is saucy. Stir in parsley. Serve over hot steaks.   *Makes 4 servings*

Nutrients per Serving (¼ of total recipe): 493 Calories, 3g Carbohydrate, 1g Dietary Fiber, 22g Total Fat, 6g Saturated Fat, 189mg Cholesterol, 474mg Sodium, 67g Protein

Grilled Steak Italiano

¾ cup CARB OPTIONS™ Italian Dressing, divided
  1 (2- to 2½-pound) T-bone, boneless sirloin or top loin steak

1. In large, shallow nonaluminum baking dish or plastic bag, pour ½ cup Carb Options Italian Dressing over steak. Cover, or close bag, and marinate in refrigerator, turning occasionally, 3 to 24 hours.

2. Remove steak from marinade; discard marinade. Grill or broil steak, turning once and brushing frequently with remaining ¼ cup Dressing, until steak is done.   *Makes 8 servings*

Preparation Time: 5 minutes
Marinate Time: 3 hours
Cook Time: 20 minutes

Nutrients per Serving (⅛ of total recipe): 210 Calories, 0g Carbohydrate, 0g Dietary Fiber, 12g Total Fat, 4g Saturated Fat, 70mg Cholesterol, 170mg Sodium, 24g Protein

Steaks with Creamy Mushroom Sauce

4 boneless sirloin steaks (about 6 ounces each)
2 tablespoons BERTOLLI® Classico Olive Oil
1 medium onion, finely chopped
1 package (10 ounces) mushrooms, thinly sliced
1 jar (1 pound) CARB OPTIONS™ Alfredo Sauce
2 teaspoons chopped fresh thyme leaves (optional)

1. Season steaks, if desired, with salt and ground black pepper. Grill or broil steaks until desired doneness.

2. Meanwhile, in 12-inch nonstick skillet, heat olive oil over medium-high heat and cook onion, stirring occasionally, 2 minutes or until tender. Add mushrooms and cook, stirring frequently, 5 minutes or until mushrooms are tender. Stir in Carb Options Alfredo Sauce and thyme and simmer 3 minutes or until heated through. Serve creamy mushroom sauce over steaks.
Makes 4 servings

Preparation Time: 10 minutes
Cook Time: 15 minutes

Nutrients per Serving ($\frac{1}{4}$ of total recipe): 490 Calories, 10g Carbohydrate, 2g Dietary Fiber, 39g Total Fat, 13g Saturated Fat, 55mg Cholesterol, 780mg Sodium, 25g Protein

Hot Tip

Never use an outdoor grill indoors, even in a tent, cabin or garage. Indoor use can create a fire hazard as well as introduce the danger of carbon monoxide fumes.

Szechuan Grilled Flank Steak

1 beef flank steak (1¼ to 1½ pounds)
¼ cup seasoned rice vinegar
¼ cup soy sauce
2 tablespoons dark sesame oil
4 cloves garlic, minced
2 teaspoons minced fresh ginger
½ teaspoon red pepper flakes
¼ cup water
½ cup thinly sliced green onions
2 to 3 teaspoons sesame seeds, toasted

1. Place steak in large resealable plastic food storage bag. Combine vinegar, soy sauce, oil, garlic, ginger and pepper flakes in small bowl; pour over steak. Press air from bag and seal; turn to coat. Marinate in refrigerator 3 hours, turning once.

2. Spray grid with nonstick cooking spray. Prepare grill for direct cooking. Drain steak; reserve marinade in small saucepan. Place steak on grid over medium heat. Grill, uncovered, 17 to 21 minutes for medium rare to medium or until desired doneness, turning once.

3. Add water to reserved marinade. Bring to a boil over high heat. Reduce heat to low; simmer 5 minutes. Transfer steak to cutting board. Slice steak across grain into thin slices. Drizzle boiled marinade over steak. Sprinkle with green onions and sesame seeds.   *Makes 4 to 6 servings*

Nutrients per Serving (¼ of total recipe): 305 Calories, 5g Carbohydrate, 1g Dietary Fiber, 17g Total Fat, 5g Saturated Fat, 70mg Cholesterol, 1174mg Sodium, 30g Protein

Szechuan Grilled Flank Steak

Peppered Beef Ribeye Roast

1½ tablespoons black peppercorns
1 boneless beef ribeye roast (about 2½ to 3 pounds), well trimmed
¼ cup Dijon mustard
2 cloves garlic, minced
Sour Cream Sauce (recipe follows)

1. Prepare grill for indirect cooking.

2. Place peppercorns in small resealable plastic food storage bag. Squeeze out excess air; close bag securely. Pound peppercorns using flat side of meat mallet or rolling pin until cracked. Set aside.

3. Pat roast dry with paper towels. Combine mustard and garlic in small bowl; spread over top and sides of roast. Sprinkle pepper over mustard mixture.

4. Place roast, pepper-side up, on grid directly over drip pan. Grill, covered, over medium heat 1 hour to 1 hour 10 minutes for medium or until internal temperature reaches 135°F for medium rare or 150°F for medium when tested with meat thermometer inserted into the thickest part of roast. Add 4 to 9 briquets to both sides of the fire after 45 minutes of cooking to maintain medium heat.

5. Meanwhile, prepare Sour Cream Sauce. Cover; refrigerate until ready to serve.

6. Transfer roast to cutting board; cover with foil. Let stand 10 to 15 minutes before carving. Internal temperature will continue to rise 5°F to 10°F during stand time. Serve with Sour Cream Sauce.

Makes 6 to 8 servings

Sour Cream Sauce

¾ cup sour cream
2 tablespoons prepared horseradish
1 tablespoon balsamic vinegar
½ teaspoon sugar

Combine all ingredients in small bowl; mix well.   *Makes about 1 cup*

Nutrients per Serving (⅙ of total recipe): 366 Calories, 4g Carbohydrate, 1g Dietary Fiber, 18g Total Fat, 8g Saturated Fat, 108mg Cholesterol, 366mg Sodium, 41g Protein

Peppered Beef Ribeye Roast

Marinated Grilled Steaks

1¼ cups orange juice
  6 tablespoons lemon juice
  6 tablespoons CRISCO® Oil*
  1 medium onion, peeled and chopped
  3 tablespoons chopped fresh parsley
1½ tablespoons bottled minced garlic *or* 2 large garlic cloves, peeled and minced
  3 bay leaves, crumbled
1½ tablespoons Italian seasoning
1½ teaspoons salt
  ¾ teaspoon freshly ground black pepper
  1 beef flank steak (2½ to 3 pounds) *or* 6 (6- to 8-ounce) beef steaks

*Use your favorite Crisco Oil product.

1. Combine orange juice, lemon juice, oil, onion, parsley, garlic, bay leaves, Italian seasoning, salt and pepper in a large resealable plastic food storage bag. Add steaks. Marinate 30 minutes to 1 hour, depending on the size of steaks and time available.

2. Prepare grill or heat broiler.

3. Remove meat from marinade. Discard marinade. Grill meat to desired doneness. Turn with tongs. Allow steaks to rest 5 minutes before carving. Serve immediately.   *Makes 6 servings*

Note: Do not marinate meat in lemon or lime juice for more than the time specified. The citric acid will turn the meat gray.

Tip: Always brush the cool grill grids with CRISCO® Oil or spray with CRISCO® No-Stick Spray before turning on the grill so that food will not stick.

Preparation Time: 10 minutes
Total Time: 1½ hours

Nutrients per Serving (⅙ of total recipe): 289 Calories, 1g Carbohydrate, <1g Dietary Fiber, 15g Total Fat, 5g Saturated Fat, 104mg Cholesterol, 136mg Sodium, 35g Protein

Asian Grilled Steaks with Spicy Herb Sauce

$2/3$ cup CRISCO® Oil*
3 tablespoons sugar
3 tablespoons cooking sherry
1 tablespoon plus $1\frac{1}{2}$ teaspoons minced garlic
1 tablespoon dark sesame oil
1 teaspoon red pepper flakes
$\frac{1}{2}$ teaspoon salt
6 (1-inch-thick) strip steaks
   Salt and black pepper, to taste

SPICY HERB SAUCE
1 cup chopped cilantro, including stems
$\frac{1}{3}$ cup CRISCO® Oil*
3 tablespoons soy sauce
1 tablespoon fresh lime juice
$1\frac{1}{2}$ teaspoons minced garlic
$\frac{1}{2}$ teaspoon dark sesame oil
$\frac{1}{2}$ teaspoon minced jalapeño pepper**

*Use your favorite Crisco Oil product.

**Jalapeño peppers can sting and irritate the skin; wear rubber gloves when handling peppers and do not touch eyes. Wash hands after handling.

1. Stir together CRISCO® Oil, sugar, sherry, garlic, sesame oil, pepper flakes and salt in a 13×9-inch baking dish. Stir until sugar is dissolved. Season steaks with salt and pepper. Add steaks, turning once to coat. Marinate for 1 hour, turning once.

2. To make Spicy Herb Sauce, stir together cilantro, CRISCO® Oil, soy sauce, lime juice, garlic, sesame oil and jalapeño; set aside.

3. Preheat grill.

4. Remove steaks from marinade. Discard marinade. Cook steaks on a medium-hot grill for 3 to 4 minutes per side for medium-rare or until desired doneness. Top each steak with sauce.   *Makes 6 servings*

Nutrients per Serving ($\frac{1}{6}$ of total recipe): 410 Calories, 3g Carbohydrate, <1g Dietary Fiber, 38g Total Fat, 9g Saturated Fat, 69mg Cholesterol, 1702mg Sodium, 15g Protein

PATIO-PERFECT PORK

Cuban Garlic & Lime Pork Chops

  6 boneless pork top loin chops, ¾ inch thick (about 1½ pounds)
  2 tablespoons olive oil
  2 tablespoons lime juice
  2 tablespoons orange juice
  2 teaspoons minced garlic
  ½ teaspoon salt, divided
  ½ teaspoon red pepper flakes
  2 small seedless oranges, peeled and chopped
  1 medium cucumber, peeled, seeded and chopped
  2 tablespoons chopped onion
  2 tablespoons chopped fresh cilantro

1. Place pork in large resealable plastic food storage bag. Add oil, juices, garlic, ¼ teaspoon salt and pepper flakes. Seal bag and shake to evenly distribute marinade; refrigerate up to 24 hours.

2. To make salsa, combine oranges, cucumber, onion and cilantro in small bowl; toss lightly. Cover and refrigerate 1 hour or overnight. Add remaining ¼ teaspoon salt just before serving.

3. To complete recipe, remove pork from marinade; discard marinade. Grill or broil pork 6 to 8 minutes on each side or until longer pink in center. Serve with salsa. *Makes 6 servings*

Nutrients per Serving (⅙ of total recipe): 201 Calories, 8g Carbohydrate, 1g Dietary Fiber, 9g Total Fat, 2g Saturated Fat, 237mg Sodium, 22g Protein

Cuban Garlic & Lime Pork Chop

Grilled Chili-Marinated Pork

3 tablespoons ground seeded dried ancho chiles*
1 teaspoon coarse or kosher salt
1/2 teaspoon ground cumin
2 tablespoons vegetable oil
1 tablespoon fresh lime juice
3 cloves garlic, minced
2 pounds pork tenderloin or thick boneless pork loin chops, trimmed of fat
Shredded romaine lettuce (optional)
Radishes for garnish

*Pasilla chiles, also known as chiles negro, are dark brown like raisins and can be substituted for ancho chiles. Mulato chiles can also be substituted.

1. Mix chiles, salt and cumin in small bowl. Stir in oil and lime juice to make smooth paste. Stir in garlic.

2. Butterfly pork by cutting lengthwise about 2/3 of the way through, leaving meat in one piece; spread meat flat. Cut tenderloin crosswise into 8 equal pieces. (If using pork chops, do not cut into pieces.)

3. Place pork between pieces of plastic wrap. Pound with flat side of meat mallet to 1/4-inch thickness.

4. Spread chili paste on both sides of pork pieces to coat evenly. Place in shallow glass baking dish. Marinate, covered, in refrigerator 2 to 3 hours.

5. Prepare coals for grill or preheat broiler. Grill or broil pork 6 inches from heat 8 to 10 minutes for grilling or 6 to 7 minutes for broiling, turning once. Serve on lettuce-lined plate. Garnish, if desired.

Makes 6 to 8 servings

Nutrients per Serving (1/6 of total recipe): 224 Calories, 2g Carbohydrate, <1g Dietary Fiber, 9g Total Fat, 2g Saturated Fat, 97mg Cholesterol, 384mg Sodium, 32g Protein

Grilled Chili-Marinated Pork

Grilled Pork Tenderloin Medallions

PEPPER & HERB RUB
  1 tablespoon garlic salt
  1 tablespoon dried basil leaves
  1 tablespoon dried thyme leaves
  1½ teaspoons cracked black pepper
  1½ teaspoons dried rosemary leaves
  1 teaspoon paprika

PORK
  2 tablespoons Pepper & Herb Rub
  12 pork tenderloin medallions (about 1 pound)
    Nonstick olive oil cooking spray

1. For rub, combine garlic salt, basil, thyme, pepper, rosemary and paprika in small jar or resealable plastic food storage bag. Store in cool dry place up to 3 months.

2. Prepare grill for direct cooking. Sprinkle rub evenly over both sides of pork; press rub lightly into pork. Spray pork with cooking spray.

3. Place pork on grid over medium-hot coals. Grill, uncovered, 4 to 5 minutes per side or until pork is no longer pink in center.

Makes 4 servings

Serving Suggestion: Serve with steamed broccoli.

Nutrients per Serving (3 Medallions): 145 Calories, 2g Carbohydrate, 1g Dietary Fiber, 4g Total Fat, 1g Saturated Fat, 66mg Cholesterol, 528mg Sodium, 24g Protein

Southwestern Kabobs

 4 boneless top loin pork chops, cut into 1-inch cubes
$^1/_4$ **cup taco or fajita seasoning**
$^1/_2$ **green bell pepper, seeded and cut into 1-inch pieces**
$^1/_2$ **large onion, peeled, cut into 1-inch pieces**

In a plastic food storage bag or shallow bowl, toss together pork cubes with taco seasoning until pork is evenly coated. Thread pork cubes, alternating with pepper and onion pieces, onto skewers.* Grill over a medium-hot fire, turning occasionally, until pork is browned.

Makes 4 servings

*If using wooden skewers, soak in water for 20 minutes before using.

Favorite recipe from **National Pork Board**

Nutrients per Serving ($^1/_4$ of total recipe): 139 Calories, 7g Carbohydrate, <1g Dietary Fiber, 2g Total Fat, <1g Saturated Fat, 51mg Cholesterol, 588mg Sodium, 21g Protein

Pork Chops Italiano

$^3/_4$ **cup CARB OPTIONS™ Italian Dressing, divided**
 4 pork chops (2 pounds), about 1 inch thick

1. In large, shallow nonaluminum baking dish or plastic bag, pour $^1/_2$ cup Carb Options Italian Dressing over chops. Cover, or close bag, and marinate in refrigerator, turning occasionally, 3 to 24 hours.

2. Remove chops from marinade, discarding marinade. Grill or broil chops, turning once and brushing frequently with remaining $^1/_4$ cup Dressing, until chops are done.

Makes 4 servings

Preparation Time: 5 minutes
Marinate Time: 3 hours
Cook Time: 20 minutes

Nutrients per Serving (1 Pork Chop): 270 Calories, 0g Carbohydrate, 0g Dietary Fiber, 14g Total Fat, 4g Saturated Fat, 90mg Cholesterol, 300mg Sodium, 34g Protein

Marinated Italian Sausage and Peppers

- ½ cup olive oil
- ¼ cup red wine vinegar
- 2 tablespoons chopped fresh parsley
- 1 tablespoon dried oregano leaves
- 2 cloves garlic, crushed
- 1 teaspoon salt
- 1 teaspoon black pepper
- 4 hot or sweet Italian sausage links
- 1 large onion, sliced into rings
- 1 large bell pepper, sliced into quarters
  Horseradish-Mustard Spread (recipe follows)

1. Combine oil, vinegar, parsley, oregano, garlic, salt and black pepper in small bowl. Place sausages, onion and bell pepper in large resealable plastic food storage bag; pour oil mixture into bag. Close bag securely; turn to coat. Marinate in refrigerator 1 to 2 hours.

2. Prepare Horseradish-Mustard Spread; set aside. Prepare grill for direct cooking. Drain sausages, onion and bell pepper; reserve marinade.

3. Grill sausages, covered, 4 to 5 minutes. Turn sausages and place onion and bell pepper on grid. Brush sausages and vegetables with reserved marinade. Grill, covered, 5 minutes or until vegetables are crisp-tender, turning vegetables halfway through grilling time. Serve sausages, onions and bell peppers with Horseradish-Mustard Spread. *Makes 4 servings*

Horseradish-Mustard Spread

- 3 tablespoons mayonnaise
- 1 tablespoon chopped fresh parsley
- 1 tablespoon prepared horseradish
- 1 tablespoon Dijon mustard
- 2 teaspoons garlic powder
- 1 teaspoon black pepper

Combine all ingredients in small bowl; mix well. *Makes about ½ cup*

Nutrients per Serving (¼ of total recipe): 610 Calories, 10g Carbohydrate, 2g Dietary Fiber, 56g Total Fat, 15g Saturated Fat, 54mg Cholesterol, 1404mg Sodium, 17g Protein

Marinated Italian Sausage and Peppers

Jerk Ribs

2 pounds pork back ribs
2 tablespoons dried minced onion
1 tablespoon plus 1 teaspoon ground thyme
1 tablespoon sugar
1 tablespoon onion powder
2 teaspoons salt
2 teaspoons ground allspice
2 teaspoons black pepper
1 teaspoon ground red pepper
$\frac{1}{2}$ teaspoon ground nutmeg
$\frac{1}{2}$ teaspoon ground cinnamon

Place all ingredients except ribs in small jar with tight-fitting lid; cover and shake until well blended. Rub dry mixture onto all surfaces of ribs.

Prepare grill with rectangular foil drip pan. Bank briquets on either side of drip pan for indirect cooking. Place ribs on grid over drip pan. Grill, on covered grill, over low coals 1$\frac{1}{2}$ hours or until ribs are tender, turning occasionally. To serve, cut into 1- or 2-rib portions.

Makes 10 servings

Conventional Directions: Prepare rub as directed. Roast ribs on rack in shallow pan in 350°F oven for 1$\frac{1}{2}$ hours or until ribs are tender.

Prep Time: 10 minutes
Cook Time: 90 minutes

Favorite recipe from **National Pork Board**

Nutrients per Serving ($\frac{1}{10}$ of total recipe): 107 Calories, 4g Carbohydrate, 1g Dietary Fiber, 8g Total Fat, 3g Saturated Fat, 27mg Cholesterol, 487mg Sodium, 6g Protein

Jerk Ribs

Glazed Pork and Pepper Kabobs

1 pound lean boneless pork loin, cut into 1½-inch pieces
1 large red bell pepper, cut into 1-inch pieces
1 large yellow bell pepper, cut into 1-inch pieces
1 large green bell pepper, cut into 1-inch pieces
¼ cup reduced-sodium soy sauce
3 cloves garlic, minced
¼ cup sweet and sour sauce
1 tablespoon Chinese hot mustard

1. Place pork and peppers in large resealable plastic food storage bag. Combine soy sauce and garlic in cup; pour over meat and peppers. Seal bag; turn to coat. Marinate in refrigerator at least 30 minutes or up to 2 hours, turning once.

2. Drain meat and peppers; discard marinade. Alternately thread meat and peppers onto 4 metal skewers.

3. Combine sweet and sour sauce and hot mustard in small bowl; reserve half of sauce mixture for dipping. Grill or broil kabobs 5 to 6 inches from heat 14 to 16 minutes or until pork is no longer pink, turning occasionally and brushing with remaining sauce mixture during last 5 minutes of cooking. Serve with reserved dipping sauce.   *Makes 4 servings*

Nutrients per Serving (1 Kabob with 1½ teaspoons dipping sauce): 230 Calories, 15g Carbohydrate, 2g Dietary Fiber, 7g Total Fat, 2g Saturated Fat, 68mg Cholesterol, 656mg Sodium, 27g Protein

August Moon Korean Ribs

⅓ cup water
⅓ cup soy sauce
¼ cup thinly sliced green onions
3 tablespoons dark sesame oil
3 tablespoons honey
2 tablespoons minced garlic
2 tablespoons sesame seeds
1 tablespoon grated fresh ginger
1 teaspoon black pepper
3½ pounds pork back ribs

To prepare marinade, combine all ingredients except ribs in small bowl. Place ribs in large resealable plastic food storage bag. Pour marinade over ribs, turning to coat. Seal bag. Marinate in refrigerator overnight. Arrange medium KINGSFORD® Briquets on each side of rectangular metal or foil drip pan. Grill ribs in center of grid on covered grill 35 to 45 minutes or until ribs are browned and cooked through, turning once.

Makes 8 servings

Nutrients per Serving (⅛ of total recipe): 429 Calories, 9g Carbohydrate, 1g Dietary Fiber, 34g Total Fat, 11g Saturated Fat, 98mg Cholesterol, 779mg Sodium, 21g Protein

Hot Tip

If you want to start cooking and the coals are too hot, use tongs to spread them. Or, remove a few of the coals and partially close the vents to slow the fire. You may also adjust the grilling rack so the food will be farther from the heat.

Tex-Mex Pork Kabobs with Chili Sour Cream Sauce

2¼ teaspoons chili powder, divided
1¾ teaspoons cumin, divided
¾ teaspoon garlic powder, divided
¾ teaspoon onion powder, divided
¾ teaspoon dried oregano leaves, divided
1 pork tenderloin (1½ pounds), trimmed and cut into 1-inch pieces
1 cup reduced-fat sour cream
¾ teaspoon salt, divided
¼ teaspoon black pepper
1 large red bell pepper, cored, seeded and cut into small chunks
1 large green bell pepper, cored, seeded and cut into small chunks
1 large yellow bell pepper, cored, seeded and cut into small chunks

1. Combine 1½ teaspoons chili powder, 1 teaspoon cumin, ½ teaspoon garlic powder, ½ teaspoon onion powder and ½ teaspoon oregano in medium bowl. Add pork; toss until well coated. Cover tightly; refrigerate 2 to 3 hours.

2. Combine sour cream, ¼ teaspoon salt, pepper and remaining ¾ teaspoon chili powder, ¾ teaspoon cumin, ¼ teaspoon garlic powder, ¼ teaspoon onion powder and ¼ teaspoon oregano in small bowl; mix well. Cover tightly; refrigerate 2 to 3 hours.

3. If using wooden skewers, soak in water 20 minutes before using. Preheat grill or broiler.

4. Toss pork with remaining ½ teaspoon salt. Thread meat and peppers onto skewers. Grill over medium-hot coals 10 minutes or until meat is no longer pink in center, turning several times. If broiling, place skewers on foil-lined baking sheet. Broil 8 inches from heat 5 minutes per side until no longer pink in center, turning once. Serve immediately with sour cream sauce. *Makes 4 to 6 servings*

Nutrients per Serving (¼ of total recipe): 320 Calories, 12g Carbohydrate, 2g Dietary Fiber, 12g Total Fat, 6g Saturated Fat, 119mg Cholesterol, 564mg Sodium, 40g Protein

Tex-Mex Pork Kabobs with Chili Sour Cream Sauce

Grilled Pork Tenderloin with Apple Salsa

1 tablespoon chili powder
$\frac{1}{2}$ teaspoon garlic powder
1 pound pork tenderloin
2 Granny Smith apples, peeled, cored and finely chopped
1 can (4 ounces) chopped green chilies
$\frac{1}{4}$ cup lemon juice
3 tablespoons finely chopped fresh cilantro
1 clove garlic, minced
1 teaspoon dried oregano leaves, crushed
$\frac{1}{2}$ teaspoon salt

1. Spray grid with nonstick cooking spray. Preheat grill to medium-high heat.

2. Combine chili and garlic powders in small bowl; mix well. Coat pork with spice mixture.

3. Grill pork 30 minutes, turning occasionally, until internal temperature reaches 165°F when tested with meat thermometer in thickest part of tenderloin. Transfer roast to cutting board; cover with foil. Let stand 10 to 15 minutes before slicing. Internal temperature will continue to rise 5°F to 10°F during stand time.

4. To make apple salsa, combine apples, chilies, lemon juice, cilantro, garlic, oregano and salt in medium bowl; mix well.

5. Slice pork across grain; serve with salsa. Garnish, if desired.

Makes 4 servings

Nutrients per Serving ($\frac{1}{4}$ of total recipe): 201 Calories, 14g Carbohydrate, 2g Dietary Fiber, 5g Total Fat, 1g Saturated Fat, 81mg Cholesterol, 678mg Sodium, 26g Protein

Grilled Pork Tenderloin With Apple Salsa

PLEASING POULTRY

Rotisserie Chicken with Pesto Brush

2 BUTTERBALL® Fresh Young Roasters
½ cup olive oil
½ cup balsamic vinegar
¼ cup chopped fresh oregano
¼ cup chopped fresh parsley
2 tablespoons chopped fresh rosemary
2 tablespoons chopped fresh thyme

Combine oil, vinegar, oregano, parsley, rosemary and thyme in small bowl. Roast chicken according to rotisserie directions. Dip brush into herb mixture; brush chicken with herb mixture every 30 minutes for first 2 hours of roasting. Brush every 15 minutes during last hour of roasting. Roast chicken until internal temperature reaches 180°F in thigh and meat is no longer pink.   *Makes 16 servings*

Tip: To make an aromatic herb brush, bundle sprigs of rosemary, thyme, oregano and parsley together. Tie bundle with kitchen string. Use as brush for pesto.

Prep Time: 15 minutes plus roasting time

Nutrients per Serving (¹⁄₁₆ of total recipe): 425 Calories, 1g Carbohydrate, <1g Dietary Fiber, 33g Total Fat, 8g Saturated Fat, 12mg Cholesterol, 114mg Sodium, 29g Protein

Rotisserie Chicken with Pesto Brush

Thai Barbecued Chicken

1 cup coarsely chopped fresh cilantro
2 jalapeño peppers,* coarsely chopped
8 cloves garlic, peeled and coarsely chopped
2 tablespoons fish sauce
1 tablespoon packed brown sugar
1 teaspoon curry powder
  Grated peel of 1 lemon
1 cut-up frying chicken (about 3 pounds)

*Jalapeño peppers can sting and irritate the skin; wear rubber gloves when handling peppers and do not touch eyes. Wash hands after handling.

1. Place cilantro, peppers, garlic, fish sauce, sugar, curry powder and lemon peel in blender or food processor; blend to form coarse paste.

2. Rinse chicken pieces; pat dry with paper towels. Work fingers between skin and meat on breast and thigh pieces. Rub about 1 teaspoon seasoning paste under skin on each piece. Rub chicken pieces on all sides with remaining paste. Place chicken in large resealable plastic food storage bag or covered container; marinate in refrigerator 3 to 4 hours or overnight.

3. Prepare grill for direct cooking. Brush grid lightly with oil. Grill chicken over medium coals, skin side down, about 10 minutes or until well browned. Turn chicken and grill 20 to 30 minutes more or until breast meat is no longer pink in center and thigh meat at bone is no longer pink. (Thighs and legs may require 10 to 15 minutes more cooking time than breasts.) If chicken is browned on both sides but still needs additional cooking, move to edge of grill, away from direct heat, to finish cooking. Garnish as desired.   *Makes 4 servings*

Nutrients per Serving (¼ of total recipe): 753 Calories, 7g Carbohydrate, 1g Dietary Fiber, 53g Total Fat, 15g Saturated Fat, 244mg Cholesterol, 925mg Sodium, 58g Protein

Thai Barbecued Chicken

Asian Grilled Chicken

  8 bamboo skewers
  4 boneless skinless chicken breast halves
  3 tablespoons low-sodium soy sauce
  3 tablespoons sesame oil
  2 tablespoons rice vinegar
  1 tablespoon MRS. DASH® Lemon Pepper seasoning
  2 teaspoons fresh minced ginger
  1 teaspoon MRS. DASH® Extra Spicy seasoning

Soak bamboo skewers in enough water to cover. Preheat grill to medium-high. Cut chicken into strips. In large shallow dish, mix soy sauce, sesame oil, vinegar, Mrs. Dash Lemon Pepper seasoning, ginger and Mrs. Dash Extra Spicy seasoning. Add chicken strips to mixture and marinate for 10 to 15 minutes. Thread chicken strips onto skewers, dividing chicken evenly. Place skewers on grill and cook for 5 minutes. Turn and brush remaining marinade over chicken; cook for 5 minutes more. Serve immediately.   *Makes 4 servings*

Preparation Time: 15 minutes
Cooking Time: 12 minutes

Nutrients per Serving (¼ of total recipe): 226 Calories, 2g Carbohydrate, 0g Dietary Fiber, 12g Total Fat, 2g Saturated Fat, 66mg Cholesterol, 438mg Sodium, 27g Protein

Classic Grilled Chicken

  1 whole frying chicken* (3½ pounds), quartered
 ¼ cup lemon juice
 ¼ cup olive oil
  2 tablespoons soy sauce
  2 large cloves garlic, minced
 ½ teaspoon sugar
 ½ teaspoon ground cumin
 ¼ teaspoon black pepper

*Substitute 3½ pounds chicken parts for whole chicken, if desired. Grill legs and thighs about 35 minutes and breast halves about 25 minutes or until chicken is no longer pink in center, turning once.

Rinse chicken under cold running water; pat dry with paper towels. Arrange chicken in 13×9×2-inch glass baking dish. Combine remaining ingredients in small bowl; pour half of mixture over chicken. Cover and refrigerate chicken at least 1 hour or overnight. Cover and reserve remaining mixture in refrigerator to use for basting. Remove chicken from marinade; discard marinade. Arrange medium KINGSFORD® Briquets on each side of large rectangular metal or foil drip pan. Pour hot tap water into drip pan until half full. Place chicken on grid directly above drip pan. Grill chicken, skin side down, on covered grill 25 minutes. Baste with reserved mixture. Turn chicken; cook 20 to 25 minutes or until juices run clear and chicken is no longer pink in center.   *Makes 6 servings*

Nutrients per Serving (⅙ of total recipe): 399 Calories, 1g Carbohydrate, <1g Dietary Fiber, 30g Total Fat, 8g Saturated Fat, 142mg Cholesterol, 298mg Sodium, 29g Protein

Turkey Teriyaki

2 tablespoons low-sodium soy sauce
2 tablespoons cooking sherry or apple juice
1 tablespoon canola oil
1 teaspoon ground ginger
1 teaspoon packed light brown sugar
1 clove garlic, minced
½ teaspoon black pepper
1 pound turkey or chicken cutlets
Additional canola oil (optional)

Combine all ingredients except turkey in small bowl; mix well. Place turkey in resealable plastic food storage bag. Pour soy sauce mixture over turkey; seal bag. Refrigerate several hours or overnight.

Remove turkey from bag; discard marinade. Grill 18 to 25 minutes or sauté in 1 teaspoon canola oil in skillet over medium heat until meat is no longer pink in center.   *Makes 4 servings*

Favorite recipe from **Canada's Canola Industry**

Nutrients per Serving (¼ of total recipe): 184 Calories, 4g Carbohydrate, 1g Dietary Fiber, 1g Total Fat, <1g Saturated Fat, 88mg Cholesterol, 160mg Sodium, 37g Protein

Chicken Tikka (Tandoori-Style Grilled Chicken)

2 chickens (3 pounds each), cut up
1 pint nonfat yogurt
1/2 cup *Frank's® RedHot®* Original Cayenne Pepper Sauce
1 tablespoon grated peeled fresh ginger
3 cloves garlic, minced
1 tablespoon paprika
1 tablespoon cumin seeds, crushed *or* 1 1/2 teaspoons ground cumin
2 teaspoons salt
1 teaspoon ground coriander

Remove skin and visible fat from chicken pieces. Rinse with cold water and pat dry. Randomly poke chicken all over with tip of sharp knife. Place chicken in resealable plastic food storage bags or large glass bowl. Combine yogurt, **Frank's RedHot** Sauce, ginger, garlic, paprika, cumin, salt and coriander in small bowl; mix well. Pour over chicken pieces, turning pieces to coat evenly. Seal bags or cover bowl and marinate in refrigerator 1 hour or overnight.

Place chicken on oiled grid, reserving marinade. Grill over medium coals 45 minutes or until chicken is no longer pink near bone and juices run clear, turning and basting often with marinade. (Do not baste during last 10 minutes of cooking.) Discard any remaining marinade. Serve warm.

Makes 6 to 8 servings

Prep Time: 15 minutes
Marinate Time: 1 hour
Cook Time: 45 minutes

Nutrients per Serving (2 pieces of chicken (1 wing or leg plus 1 thigh or breast)): 746 Calories, 8g Carbohydrate, 1g Dietary Fiber, 50g Total Fat, 14g Saturated Fat, 238mg Cholesterol, 1145mg Sodium, 61g Protein

Chicken Tikka (Tandoori-Style Grilled Chicken)

Spicy Island Chicken

1 cup finely chopped white onion
$\frac{1}{3}$ cup white wine vinegar
6 green onions, finely chopped
6 cloves garlic, minced
1 habañero or serrano pepper,* finely chopped
3 tablespoons plus 1$\frac{1}{2}$ teaspoons fresh thyme *or* 2 teaspoons dried
    thyme leaves
3 tablespoons plus 1$\frac{1}{2}$ teaspoons olive oil
1 tablespoon ground allspice
2 teaspoons sugar
1 teaspoon salt
1 teaspoon ground cinnamon
1 teaspoon ground nutmeg
1 teaspoon black pepper
$\frac{1}{2}$ teaspoon ground red pepper
6 boneless skinless chicken breasts

*Habañero peppers can sting and irritate the skin; wear rubber gloves when handling peppers and do not touch eyes. Wash hands after handling.

1. Combine all ingredients except chicken in medium bowl; mix well. Place chicken in resealable plastic food storage bag and add seasoning mixture. Seal bag; turn to coat chicken. Marinate in refrigerator 4 hours or overnight.

2. Spray cold grid with nonstick cooking spray. Adjust grid to 4 to 6 inches above heat. Preheat grill to medium-high heat.

3. Grill chicken 5 to 7 minutes per side or until no longer pink in center, brushing occasionally with marinade. *Do not brush with marinade during last 5 minutes of grilling.* Discard remaining marinade.

Makes 6 servings

Nutrients per Serving (1 Chicken breast): 164 Calories, 3g Carbohydrate, 1g Dietary Fiber, 5g Total Fat, 1g Saturated Fat, 69mg Cholesterol, 256mg Sodium, 26g Protein

Grilled Chicken au Poivre Salad

    4 boneless skinless chicken breasts (about 1¼ pounds)
  ¼ cup finely chopped onion
2½ tablespoons white wine vinegar, divided
  ¼ cup plus 3 tablespoons olive oil, divided
    2 teaspoons cracked or coarse ground black pepper
  ½ teaspoon salt
  ¼ teaspoon poultry seasoning
    3 cloves garlic, minced
    1 tablespoon Dijon mustard
      Dash sugar
    1 bag (10 ounces) prewashed salad greens
    2 cherry tomatoes, halved

1. Place chicken, onion, 1 tablespoon vinegar, ¼ cup oil, pepper, salt, poultry seasoning and garlic in resealable plastic food storage bag. Seal bag; knead to coat chicken. Refrigerate at least 2 hours or overnight.

2. Grill chicken, covered, over medium-hot coals 10 to 15 minutes or until no longer pink in center.

3. For dressing, combine remaining 1½ tablespoons vinegar, 3 tablespoons oil, mustard and sugar in small bowl; whisk until smooth.

4. Arrange salad greens and cherry tomatoes on 4 plates.

5. Cut chicken crosswise into strips. Arrange strips on top of greens. Drizzle with dressing.   *Makes 4 servings*

Nutrients per Serving (¼ of total recipe): 252 Calories, 5g Carbohydrate, 2g Dietary Fiber, 15g Total Fat, 2g Saturated Fat, 53mg Cholesterol, 439mg Sodium, 23g Protein

Asian Chicken Kabobs

1 pound boneless skinless chicken breasts, cut into 1½-inch pieces
2 small zucchini or yellow squash, cut into 1-inch slices
8 large fresh mushrooms
1 cup red, yellow or green bell pepper pieces
2 tablespoons reduced-sodium soy sauce
2 tablespoons dry sherry
1 teaspoon dark sesame oil
2 cloves garlic, minced
2 large green onions, cut into 1-inch pieces

1. Place chicken in large resealable plastic food storage bag. Add zucchini, mushrooms and bell pepper to bag. Combine soy sauce, sherry, oil and garlic in small bowl; pour over chicken and vegetables. Close bag securely; turn to coat. Marinate in refrigerator at least 30 minutes or up to 4 hours.

2. Soak 4 (12-inch) wooden skewers in water 20 minutes.

3. Drain chicken and vegetables; reserve marinade. Alternately thread chicken and vegetables with onions onto skewers.

4. Prepare grill for direct cooking.

5. Brush prepared skewers with half of reserved marinade. Grill 5 to 6 inches from heat 5 minutes. Turn kabobs over; brush with remaining marinade. Grill 5 minutes more or until chicken is no longer pink. Garnish with green onion brushes, if desired. *Makes 4 servings*

Nutrients per Serving (1 Kabob): 135 Calories, 6g Carbohydrate, 2g Dietary Fiber, 3g Total Fat, 1g Saturated Fat, 46mg Cholesterol, 307mg Sodium, 19g Protein

Cajun Grilled Chicken

4 boneless skinless chicken breast halves (4 ounces each)
2 tablespoons lemon juice
3 tablespoons MRS. DASH® Extra Spicy Seasoning
2 tablespoons paprika
1 tablespoon brown sugar
Cooking spray

Preheat grill to medium high. With a sharp knife, slash each piece of chicken in 2 or 3 places with ¼-inch-deep cuts. In a bowl, combine chicken and lemon juice, turning the chicken until it is thoroughly coated. Set aside. In separate bowl, mix Mrs. Dash Extra Spicy seasoning, paprika and brown sugar. Take each piece of chicken and roll in the spice mixture until well coated. Spray grill with cooking spray and place seasoned chicken breasts on the grill. Cook 5 minutes, turn, and cook 5 minutes more or until juices run clear when a skewer is inserted. Serve immediately.   *Makes 4 servings*

Preparation Time: 10 minutes
Cooking Time: 10 minutes

Nutrients per Serving (1 Grilled Chicken breast half): 148 Calories, 6g Carbohydrate, 1g Dietary Fiber, 2g Total Fat, <1g Saturated Fat, 66mg Cholesterol, 61mg Sodium, 27g Protein

South of the Border Turkey Kabobs

1 package BUTTERBALL® Fresh Boneless Turkey Breast Medallions
¼ cup vegetable oil
¼ cup fresh lime juice
2 teaspoons salt
1 teaspoon chili powder
½ teaspoon garlic powder
2 medium yellow squash, cut into ¾-inch chunks
2 medium onions, cut into ¾-inch chunks
2 red bell peppers, cut into ¾-inch chunks
2 green bell peppers, cut into ¾-inch chunks

Combine oil, lime juice, salt, chili powder and garlic powder in large bowl. Toss vegetables in oil mixture; stir to coat. Transfer vegetables to separate large bowl. Add turkey medallions to oil mixture; stir to coat. Thread turkey and vegetables alternately onto skewers, leaving small space between pieces. Grill over hot coals about 20 minutes or until turkey is no longer pink in center, turning occasionally to prevent burning.
Makes 6 servings

Prep Time: 30 minutes

Nutrients per Serving (⅙ of total recipe): 165 Calories, 11g Carbohydrate, 3g Dietary Fiber, 10g Total Fat, 1g Saturated Fat, 25mg Cholesterol, 760mg Sodium, 11g Protein

Hot Tip

For the best kabobs, parboil solid or starchy vegetables, such as carrots or potatoes, before placing them on the grill.

Spiced Turkey with Fruit Salsa

6 ounces turkey breast tenderloin
2 teaspoons lime juice
1 teaspoon mesquite seasoning blend or ground cumin
½ cup canned or frozen pitted sweet cherries, thawed and cut into
    halves
¼ cup chunky salsa

Prepare grill for direct cooking. Brush both sides of turkey with lime juice. Sprinkle with mesquite seasoning. Grill turkey over medium coals 15 to 20 minutes or until no longer pink in center and juices run clear, turning once. Meanwhile, stir together cherries and salsa. Slice turkey. Spoon salsa mixture over turkey.   *Makes 2 servings*

Nutrients per Serving (½ of total recipe): 125 Calories, 11g Carbohydrate, 2g Dietary Fiber, 2g Total Fat, 1g Saturated Fat, 34mg Cholesterol, 264mg Sodium, 16g Protein

Grilled Chicken with Chimichurri Salsa

4 boneless skinless chicken breasts (6 ounces each)
½ cup plus 4 teaspoons olive oil
  Salt and black pepper
½ cup finely chopped parsley
¼ cup white wine vinegar
2 tablespoons finely chopped onion
3 cloves garlic, minced
1 jalapeño pepper,* finely chopped
2 teaspoons dried oregano leaves

*Jalapeño peppers can sting and irritate the skin; wear rubber gloves when handling peppers and do not touch eyes. Wash hands after handling.

1. Prepare grill for direct cooking. Brush chicken with 4 teaspoons olive oil; season with salt and black pepper. Place on oiled grid. Grill, covered, over medium heat 5 to 8 minutes on each side or until chicken is no longer pink in center.

2. To prepare salsa, combine parsley, vinegar, onion, garlic, jalapeño pepper, oregano, remaining ½ cup olive oil, and salt and pepper to taste. Serve over chicken.   *Makes 4 servings*

Nutrients per Serving (¼ of total recipe): 577 Calories, 3g Carbohydrate, <1g Dietary Fiber, 46g Total Fat, 8g Saturated Fat, 108mg Cholesterol, 382mg Sodium, 36g Protein

Spiced Turkey with Fruit Salsa

Mustard Grilled Chicken with Dipping Sauce

$\frac{1}{2}$ cup **CARB OPTIONS**™ Whipped Dressing
2 green onions, chopped
2 tablespoons mustard
1 teaspoon apple cider vinegar
$\frac{1}{8}$ teaspoon ground black pepper
   Pinch salt
4 boneless, skinless chicken breast halves (about 1 pound)

1. In medium bowl, combine all ingredients except chicken. Reserve $\frac{1}{3}$ cup mixture.

2. Grill or broil chicken, brushing frequently with remaining mixture, 12 minutes or until chicken is thoroughly cooked, turning once. Serve chicken with $\frac{1}{3}$ cup reserved mixture and garnish, if desired, with additional chopped green onions.   *Makes 4 servings*

Preparation Time: 10 minutes
Cook Time: 12 minutes

Nutrients per Serving ($\frac{1}{4}$ of total recipe): 240 Calories, 2g Carbohydrate, 0g Dietary Fiber, 14g Total Fat, 3g Saturated Fat, 80mg Cholesterol, 360mg Sodium, 25g Protein

Hot Tip

Chicken breasts, the white meat of chicken, are a popular cut. Recipe reference to chicken breasts usually means a chicken breast half. Studies have shown that the breast is juicier if cooked with the skin attached. After removing and discarding the skin, the chicken does not have any more fat than chicken cooked without the skin.

Thai Grilled Chicken

4 boneless chicken breast halves, skinned if desired (about
   1¼ pounds)
¼ cup soy sauce
2 teaspoons minced garlic
½ teaspoon red pepper flakes
2 tablespoons honey
1 tablespoon fresh lime juice

1. Prepare grill for direct cooking. Place chicken in shallow baking dish.
Combine soy sauce, garlic and pepper flakes in small bowl. Pour over
chicken, turning to coat. Let stand 10 minutes.

2. Meanwhile, combine honey and lime juice in small bowl until blended;
set aside.

3. Place chicken on grid over medium coals; brush with marinade.
Discard remaining marinade. Grill, covered, 5 minutes. Brush both sides
of chicken with honey mixture. Grill 5 minutes more or until chicken is
cooked through.   *Makes 4 servings*

Serving Suggestion: Serve with Oriental vegetables and a fresh green
salad.

Prep and Cook Time: 25 minutes

Nutrients per Serving (¼ of total recipe): 146 Calories, 11g Carbohydrate,
<1g Dietary Fiber, 1g Total Fat, <1g Saturated Fat, 53mg Cholesterol,
1077mg Sodium, 22g Protein

Orange Vinaigrette Grilled Chicken Salad

1¼ cups prepared fat-free red wine vinaigrette salad dressing
¼ cup MRS. DASH® Lemon Pepper Seasoning
1 pound boneless, skinless chicken breast halves
1 bunch romaine lettuce, torn
1 (11-ounce) can mandarin oranges, drained
Chopped fresh vegetables of your choice

Whisk together salad dressing and Mrs. Dash Lemon Pepper seasoning. Reserve ¾ cup mixture. Brush chicken with remaining ½ cup dressing mixture. Grill, turning and brushing occasionally, until chicken is no longer pink in center, about 15 to 20 minutes. Cut chicken into strips. Serve over lettuce with oranges and desired vegetables. Drizzle reserved dressing over salad. *Makes 4 servings*

Preparation Time: 5 minutes
Cooking Time: 20 minutes

Nutrients per Serving (¼ of total recipe): 165 Calories, 9g Carbohydrate, 2g Dietary Fiber, 2g Total Fat, <1g Saturated Fat, 66mg Cholesterol, 1020mg Sodium, 28g Protein

Grilled Chicken

1 (2½- to 3-pound) chicken, cut into serving pieces
1 cup CARB OPTIONS™ Original Barbecue Sauce

Grill or broil chicken, brushing frequently with Carb Options Original Barbecue Sauce, until chicken is thoroughly cooked.
Makes 4 servings

Preparation Time: 5 minutes
Cook Time: 25 minutes

Nutrients per Serving (2 Chicken pieces): 280 Calories, 3g Carbohydrate, 1g Dietary Fiber, 15g Total Fat, 4g Saturated Fat, 95mg Cholesterol, 770mg Sodium, 30g Protein

Mixed Grill

2 fennel bulbs
1 large red bell pepper
3 baby Japanese white eggplants *or* 2 small purple eggplants
3 plum tomatoes
3 large portobello mushrooms, wiped clean and stems removed
4 tablespoons light vinaigrette salad dressing
1 package (4 links) precooked chicken and apple sausages
10 ounces boneless, skinless chicken tenders
   Black pepper
1 tablespoon fresh minced parsley

1. Preheat grill to 400°F. Soak 8 wooden skewers in water 20 minutes. Slice fennel lengthwise. Cut red pepper into large chunks. Cut eggplant, tomatoes and mushroom caps into thick slices.

2. Thread vegetables onto skewers; sprinkle with salad dressing.

3. Slice sausages lengthwise; set aside. Remove chicken from package. Sprinkle with lemon pepper and black pepper; set aside.

4. Place vegetable skewers, chicken sausages and chicken tenders on grill. Cook 5 to 10 minutes, or until chicken reaches an internal temperature of 160°F. Sprinkle with parsley and serve.   *Makes 8 servings*

Nutrients per Serving (1 vegetable skewer, 1 piece of sausage and 1¼ ounces of chicken tenders): 91 Calories, 8g Carbohydrate, 3g Dietary Fiber, 3g Total Fat, <1g Saturated Fat, 22mg Cholesterol, 437mg Sodium, 9g Protein

SIZZLING SEAFOOD

Szechuan Tuna Steaks

  4 tuna steaks (6 ounces each), cut 1 inch thick
$\frac{1}{4}$ cup dry sherry or sake
$\frac{1}{4}$ cup soy sauce
  1 tablespoon dark sesame oil
  1 teaspoon hot chili oil*
  1 clove garlic, minced
  3 tablespoons chopped fresh cilantro

*If hot chili oil is not available, combine 1 teaspoon vegetable oil and $\frac{1}{4}$ teaspoon red pepper flakes in small microwavable cup. Microwave at HIGH 30 to 45 seconds. Let stand 5 minutes to allow flavor to develop.

1. Place tuna in single layer in large shallow glass dish. Combine sherry, soy sauce, sesame oil, chili oil and garlic in small bowl. Reserve $\frac{1}{4}$ cup soy sauce mixture at room temperature. Pour remaining soy sauce mixture over tuna. Cover; marinate in refrigerator 40 minutes, turning once.

2. Spray grid with nonstick cooking spray. Prepare grill for direct cooking. Drain tuna; discard marinade. Place tuna on grid. Grill, uncovered, over medium-hot coals 6 minutes or until tuna is opaque, but still feels somewhat soft in center,** turning halfway through grilling time. Transfer tuna to cutting board. Cut each tuna steak into thin slices; fan out slices onto serving plates. Drizzle tuna slices with reserved soy sauce mixture; sprinkle with cilantro.

Makes 4 servings

**Tuna becomes dry and tough if overcooked. Cook it as if it were beef.

Nutrients per Serving (1 Steak with 1 tablespoon sauce): 284 Calories, 2g Carbohydrate, <1g Dietary Fiber, 11g Total Fat, 2g Saturated Fat, 62mg Cholesterol, 631mg Sodium, 40g Protein

Szechuan Tuna Steak

Hot Shrimp with Cool Salsa

¼ **cup prepared salsa**
4 **tablespoons fresh lime juice, divided**
1 **teaspoon honey**
1 **clove garlic, minced**
2 **to 4 drops hot pepper sauce**
1 **pound large shrimp, peeled and deveined, with tails intact**
1 **cup finely diced honeydew melon**
½ **cup finely diced unpeeled cucumber**
2 **tablespoons minced parsley**
1 **green onion, finely chopped**
1½ **teaspoons sugar**
1 **teaspoon olive oil**
¼ **teaspoon salt**

1. To make marinade, combine prepared salsa, 2 tablespoons lime juice, honey, garlic and hot pepper sauce in small bowl. Thread shrimp onto skewers. Brush shrimp with marinade; set aside.

2. To make salsa, combine remaining 2 tablespoons lime juice, melon, cucumber, parsley, onion, sugar, oil and salt in medium bowl; mix well.

3. Grill shrimp over medium coals 4 to 5 minutes or until shrimp are opaque, turning once. Serve with salsa.   *Makes 4 servings*

Nutrients per Serving (¼ of total recipe): 132 Calories, 8g Carbohydrate, 1g Dietary Fiber, 2g Total Fat, <1g Saturated Fat, 175mg Cholesterol, 398mg Sodium, 19g Protein

Hot Tip

Shrimp may be peeled and deveined either before or after they are cooked. If cooked, peel and devein them while still warm. The shell is easily removed with your fingers. Start to peel it off on the side with the legs. Lift it up and over, then back around the leg side. The tail section may be removed or left intact.

Hot Shrimp with Cool Salsa

Mustard-Grilled Red Snapper

   ½ cup Dijon mustard
   1 tablespoon red wine vinegar
   1 teaspoon ground red pepper
   4 red snapper fillets (about 6 ounces each)
      Fresh parsley sprigs and red peppercorns (optional)

1. Spray grid with nonstick cooking spray. Prepare grill for direct cooking.

2. Combine mustard, vinegar and pepper in small bowl; mix well. Coat fish thoroughly with mustard mixture.

3. Place fish on grid. Grill, covered, over medium-high heat 8 minutes or until fish flakes easily when tested with fork, turning halfway through grilling time. Garnish with parsley sprigs and red peppercorns, if desired.

Makes 4 servings

Nutrients per Serving (1 Snapper fillet): 210 Calories, 4g Carbohydrate, 1g Dietary Fiber, 5g Total Fat, 1g Saturated Fat, 63mg Cholesterol, 246mg Sodium, 37g Protein

Shrimp and Pineapple Kabobs

    8 ounces medium shrimp, peeled and deveined
   ½ cup pineapple juice
   ¼ teaspoon garlic powder
   12 chunks canned pineapple
    1 green bell pepper, cut into 1-inch pieces
   ¼ cup prepared chili sauce

1. Combine shrimp, juice and garlic powder in bowl; toss to coat. Marinate in refrigerator 30 minutes. Drain shrimp; discard marinade.

2. Prepare grill for direct cooking. Alternately thread pineapple, pepper and shrimp onto 4 (10-inch) skewers. Brush with chili sauce. Grill, 4 inches from hot coals, 5 minutes or until shrimp are opaque, turning once and basting with chili sauce.

Makes 4 servings

Nutrients per Serving (1 Kabob): 100 Calories, 14g Carbohydrate, 1g Dietary Fiber, <1g Total Fat, <1g Saturated Fat, 87mg Cholesterol, 302mg Sodium, 10g Protein

Mustard-Grilled Red Snapper

Grilled Red Snapper with Avocado-Papaya Salsa

1 teaspoon ground coriander seed
1 teaspoon paprika
¾ teaspoon salt
⅛ to ¼ teaspoon ground red pepper
1 tablespoon olive oil
4 skinless red snapper or halibut fish fillets (5 to 7 ounces each)
½ cup diced ripe avocado
½ cup diced ripe papaya
2 tablespoons chopped fresh cilantro
1 tablespoon fresh lime juice
4 lime wedges

1. Prepare grill for direct cooking. Combine coriander, paprika, salt and red pepper in small bowl or cup; mix well.

2. Brush oil over fish. Sprinkle 2½ teaspoons spice mixture over fish fillets; set aside remaining spice mixture. Place fish on oiled grid over medium-hot heat. Grill 5 minutes per side or until fish is opaque.

3. Meanwhile, combine avocado, papaya, cilantro, lime juice and reserved spice mixture in medium bowl; mix well. Serve fish with salsa and garnish with lime wedges.

Makes 4 servings

Nutrients per Serving (¼ of total recipe): 221 Calories, 5g Carbohydrate, 2g Dietary Fiber, 9g Total Fat, <1g Saturated Fat, 51mg Cholesterol, 559mg Sodium, 30g Protein

Grilled Red Snapper with Avocado-Papaya Salsa

Marinated Salmon with Lemon Tarragon Sauce

1/4 cup lemon juice
1/4 cup olive oil
2 cloves garlic, crushed
3/4 teaspoon salt, divided
1/4 teaspoon black pepper
1 pound fresh 1-inch-thick salmon fillet
2/3 cup sour cream
1/4 cup minced green onions
1/4 cup milk
1 tablespoon fresh tarragon *or* 1 teaspoon dried tarragon leaves

1. Combine lemon juice, oil, garlic, 1/2 teaspoon salt and pepper in shallow, nonreactive 11×7-inch baking dish. Mix well. Add salmon; turn twice to coat with marinade. With salmon skin-side up in baking dish, cover tightly; refrigerate 2 hours.

2. Combine sour cream, green onions, milk, tarragon and remaining 1/4 teaspoon salt in small bowl; mix well. Cover; refrigerate until ready to serve.

3. Cut salmon into 4 pieces. Preheat grill or broiler. If grilling, cook over medium-hot coals 5 minutes per side or until fish begins to flake when tested with fork. If broiling, place skin side down on broiling pan. Cook 6 inches from heat 8 to 10 minutes or until fish just begins to flake when tested with fork. Serve hot with chilled sauce.   *Makes 4 servings*

Nutrients per Serving (1/4 of total recipe): 294 Calories, 3g Carbohydrate, <1g Dietary Fiber, 20g Total Fat, 8g Saturated Fat, 71mg Cholesterol, 253mg Sodium, 24g Protein

Marinated Salmon with Lemon Tarragon Sauce

Grilled Five-Spice Fish with Garlic Spinach

1½ teaspoons grated lime peel
3 tablespoons fresh lime juice
1 tablespoon plus 1 teaspoon minced fresh ginger
2 teaspoons vegetable oil, divided
½ to 1 teaspoon Chinese five-spice powder*
½ teaspoon sugar
½ teaspoon salt
⅛ teaspoon black pepper
1 pound salmon steaks
½ pound fresh baby spinach leaves (about 8 cups lightly packed), washed
2 large cloves garlic, pressed through garlic press

*Chinese five-spice powder is available in most supermarkets and at Asian grocery stores.

1. Combine lime peel, lime juice, ginger, 1 teaspoon oil, five-spice powder, sugar, salt and pepper in 2-quart dish. Add salmon; turn to coat. Cover; refrigerate 2 to 3 hours.

2. Combine spinach, garlic and remaining 1 teaspoon oil in 3-quart microwavable dish; toss. Cover; microwave at HIGH 2 minutes or until spinach is wilted. Drain; keep warm.

3. Meanwhile, prepare grill for direct cooking.

4. Remove salmon from marinade and place on oiled grid. Brush salmon with marinade. Grill salmon, covered, over medium-hot coals 4 minutes. Turn salmon; brush with marinade and grill 4 minutes or until fish begins to flake with fork. Discard remaining marinade.

5. Serve fish over bed of spinach.   *Makes 4 servings*

Nutrients per Serving (¼ of total recipe): 133 Calories, 4g Carbohydrate, 2g Dietary Fiber, 3g Total Fat, <1g Saturated Fat, 49mg Cholesterol, 405mg Sodium, 22g Protein

Grilled Five-Spice Fish with Garlic Spinach

Lobster Tail with Tasty Butters

Hot & Spicy Butter, Scallion Butter or Chili-Mustard Butter (recipes
   follow)
4 fresh or thawed frozen lobster tails (about 5 ounces each)

1. Prepare grill for direct cooking. Prepare 1 butter mixture.

2. Rinse lobster tails in cold water. Butterfly tails by cutting lengthwise
through centers of hard top shells and meat. Cut to, but not through,
bottoms of shells. Press shell halves of tails apart with fingers. Brush
lobster meat with butter mixture.

3. Place tails on grid, meat side down. Grill, uncovered, over medium-
high heat 4 minutes. Turn tails meat side up. Brush with butter mixture;
grill 4 to 5 minutes or until lobster meat turns opaque.

4. Heat remaining butter mixture, stirring occasionally. Serve butter sauce
for dipping.   *Makes 4 servings*

Tasty Butters

HOT & SPICY BUTTER
   $1/3$ cup butter or margarine, melted
   1 tablespoon chopped onion
   2 to 3 teaspoons hot pepper sauce
   1 teaspoon dried thyme leaves
   $1/4$ teaspoon ground allspice

SCALLION BUTTER
   $1/3$ cup butter or margarine, melted
   1 tablespoon finely chopped green onion tops
   1 tablespoon lemon juice
   1 teaspoon grated lemon peel
   $1/4$ teaspoon black pepper

CHILI-MUSTARD BUTTER
   $1/3$ cup butter or margarine, melted
   1 tablespoon chopped onion
   1 tablespoon Dijon mustard
   1 teaspoon chili powder

For each butter sauce, combine ingredients in small bowl.

continued on page 74

Lobster Tail with Hot & Spicy Butter

Lobster Tail with Tasty Butters, continued

Nutrients per Serving (1 Lobster Tail with about 2 tablespoons Butter):
278 Calories, 1g Carbohydrate, <1g Dietary Fiber, 18g Total Fat, 8g Saturated Fat,
178mg Cholesterol, 628mg Sodium, 27g Protein

Grilled Scallops and Vegetables with Cilantro Sauce

1 teaspoon hot chili oil*
1 teaspoon dark sesame oil
1 green onion, chopped
1 tablespoon finely chopped fresh ginger
1 cup fat-free reduced-sodium chicken broth
1 cup chopped fresh cilantro
1 pound raw or thawed frozen sea scallops
2 medium zucchini, cut into ½-inch slices
2 medium yellow squash, cut into ½-inch slices
1 medium yellow onion, cut into wedges
8 large mushrooms

*If hot chili oil is not available, combine 1 teaspoon vegetable oil and
¼ teaspoon red pepper flakes in small microwavable cup. Microwave at
HIGH 30 to 45 seconds. Let stand 5 minutes to allow flavor to develop.

1. Spray cold grid with nonstick cooking spray. Preheat grill to medium-
high heat. Heat chili oil and sesame oil in small saucepan over medium-
low heat. Add green onion; cook about 15 seconds or just until fragrant.
Add ginger; cook 1 minute.

2. Add chicken broth; bring mixture to a boil. Cook until liquid is reduced
by half. Cool slightly. Place mixture in blender or food processor with
cilantro; blend until smooth. Set aside.

3. Thread scallops and vegetables onto 4 (12-inch) skewers. (If using
wooden skewers, soak in water 20 minutes before using to prevent
burning.) Grill about 8 minutes per side or until scallops turn opaque.
Serve hot with cilantro sauce. Garnish, if desired.   *Makes 4 servings*

Nutrients per Serving (1 skewer): 194 Calories, 11g Carbohydrate, 3g Dietary Fiber,
7g Total Fat, <1g Saturated Fat, 36mg Cholesterol, 644mg Sodium, 23g Protein

Grilled Scallops and Vegetables with Cilantro Sauce

Seafood Kabobs

 1 pound uncooked large shrimp, peeled and deveined
10 ounces skinless swordfish or halibut steaks, cut 1 inch thick
 2 tablespoons honey mustard
 2 teaspoons fresh lemon juice
 8 slices bacon (regular thickness)
   Lemon wedges and fresh herbs (optional)

1. Spray grid with nonstick cooking spray. Prepare grill for direct cooking.

2. Place shrimp in shallow glass dish. Cut swordfish into 1-inch cubes; add to dish. Combine mustard and lemon juice in small bowl. Pour over seafood; toss lightly to coat.

3. Pierce one 12-inch metal skewer through 1 end of bacon slice. Add 1 piece shrimp. Pierce skewer through bacon slice again, wrapping bacon slice around 1 side of shrimp. Add 1 piece swordfish. Pierce bacon slice again, wrapping bacon around opposite side of swordfish. Continue adding seafood and wrapping with bacon, pushing ingredients to middle of skewer until end of bacon slice is reached. Repeat with 7 more skewers.

4. Brush any remaining mustard mixture over skewers; place skewers on grid. Grill, covered, over medium heat 8 to 10 minutes or until shrimp are opaque and swordfish flakes easily when tested with fork, turning halfway through grilling time. Garnish with lemon wedges and fresh herbs, if desired. *Makes 4 servings*

Note: Kabobs can be prepared up to 3 hours before grilling. Cover and refrigerate until ready to grill.

Nutrients per Serving (2 Kabobs): 305 Calories, 3g Carbohydrate, <1g Dietary Fiber, 12g Total Fat, 4g Saturated Fat, 214mg Cholesterol, 514mg Sodium, 37g Protein

Seafood Kabobs

Grilled Salmon Fillets, Asparagus and Onions

½ teaspoon paprika
6 salmon fillets (6 to 8 ounces each)
⅓ cup bottled honey-Dijon marinade or barbecue sauce
1 bunch (about 1 pound) fresh asparagus spears, ends trimmed
1 large red or sweet onion, cut into ¼-inch slices
1 tablespoon olive oil
   Salt and black pepper

1. Prepare grill for direct cooking. Sprinkle paprika over salmon fillets. Brush marinade over salmon; let stand at room temperature 15 minutes.

2. Brush asparagus and onion slices with olive oil; season to taste with salt and pepper.

3. Place salmon, skin side down, in center of grid over medium coals. Arrange asparagus spears and onion slices around salmon. Grill salmon and vegetables on covered grill 5 minutes. Turn salmon, asparagus and onion slices. Grill 5 to 6 minutes more or until salmon flakes when tested with a fork and vegetables are crisp-tender. Separate onion slices into rings; arrange over asparagus. *Makes 6 servings*

Prep and Cook Time: 26 minutes

Nutrients per Serving (⅙ of total recipe): 255 Calories, 8g Carbohydrate, 2g Dietary Fiber, 8g Total Fat, 1g Saturated Fat, 86mg Cholesterol, 483mg Sodium, 35g Protein

Hot Tip

Although salmon has a higher fat content than most fish, it is still very nutritious. Salmon's fat content is made up primarily of omega-3 fatty acids. There is a wealth of research available today that links consumption of omega-3 fatty acids with the reduced risk of heart attack and heart disease.

Grilled Salmon Fillet, Asparagus and Onions

Mesquite-Grilled Salmon Fillets

2 tablespoons olive oil
1 clove garlic, minced
2 tablespoons lemon juice
1 teaspoon grated lemon peel
½ teaspoon dried dill weed
½ teaspoon dried thyme leaves
¼ teaspoon salt
¼ teaspoon black pepper
4 salmon fillets, ¾ to 1 inch thick (about 5 ounces each)

1. Cover 1 cup mesquite chips with cold water; soak 20 to 30 minutes. Spray grid with nonstick cooking spray. Prepare grill for direct cooking.

2. Combine oil and garlic in small microwavable bowl. Microwave at HIGH 1 minute or until garlic is tender. Add lemon juice, lemon peel, dill, thyme, salt and pepper; whisk until blended. Brush skinless sides of salmon with half of lemon mixture.

3. Drain mesquite chips; sprinkle chips over coals. Place salmon, skin side up, on grid. Grill, covered, over medium-high heat 4 to 5 minutes; turn and brush with remaining lemon mixture. Grill 4 to 5 minutes more or until salmon flakes easily when tested with fork.   *Makes 4 servings*

Nutrients per Serving (1 Salmon Fillet): 322 Calories, 1g Carbohydrate, <1g Dietary Fiber, 22g Total Fat, 4g Saturated Fat, 83mg Cholesterol, 230mg Sodium, 28g Protein

Mesquite-Grilled Salmon Fillet

Grilled Swordfish á l'Orange

   4 swordfish, halibut or shark steaks (about 1½ pounds)
   1 orange
   ¾ cup orange juice
   1 tablespoon lemon juice
   1 tablespoon dark sesame oil
   1 tablespoon soy sauce
   1 teaspoon cornstarch
      Salt and black pepper

1. Rinse swordfish and pat dry with paper towels. Grate enough orange peel to measure 1 teaspoon; set aside. Peel orange and cut into sections; set aside. Combine orange juice, lemon juice, oil and soy sauce in small bowl. Pour half of orange juice mixture into shallow glass dish; add ½ teaspoon grated orange peel to orange juice mixture. Add fish; turn to coat in mixture. Cover; marinate in refrigerator up to 1 hour.

2. Prepare grill for direct cooking.

3. Place remaining half of orange juice mixture in small saucepan. Stir in cornstarch and remaining ½ teaspoon orange peel. Heat over medium-high heat, stirring constantly, 3 to 5 minutes or until sauce thickens; set aside.

4. Remove fish from marinade; discard remaining marinade. Lightly season fish with salt and pepper. Grill over medium coals 3 to 4 minutes per side or until fish is opaque and flakes easily when tested with fork. Top with reserved orange sections and orange sauce. Serve immediately.

Makes 4 servings

Nutrients per Serving (¼ of total recipe): 276 Calories, 12g Carbohydrate, 2g Dietary Fiber, 10g Total Fat, 2g Saturated Fat, 65mg Cholesterol, 412mg Sodium, 35g Protein

SMOKING SIDES

Grilled Vegetables

¼ cup minced fresh herbs, such as parsley, thyme, rosemary, oregano or basil
1 small eggplant (about ¾ pound), cut into ¼-inch-thick slices
½ teaspoon salt
1 *each* red, green and yellow bell peppers, quartered and seeded
2 zucchini, cut lengthwise into ¼-inch-thick slices
1 fennel bulb, cut lengthwise into ¼-inch-thick slices
Nonstick cooking spray

1. Combine herbs in small bowl; let stand 3 hours or overnight.

2. Place eggplant in large colander over bowl; sprinkle with salt. Drain 1 hour.

3. Prepare grill for direct cooking. Spray vegetables with cooking spray and sprinkle with herb mixture. Grill over high heat 10 to 15 minutes or until fork-tender and lightly browned on both sides. (Cooking times vary depending on vegetable; remove vegetables as they are done, to avoid overcooking.) *Makes 6 servings*

Variation: Cut vegetables into 1-inch cubes and thread onto skewers. Spray with cooking spray and sprinkle with herb mixture. Grill as directed above.

Nutrients per Serving (⅙ of total recipe): 34 Calories, 8g Carbohydrate, 2g Dietary Fiber, <1g Total Fat, <1g Saturated Fat, 0mg Cholesterol, 190mg Sodium, 1g Protein

Herbed Mushroom Vegetable Medley

4 ounces button or crimini mushrooms
1 medium red or yellow bell pepper, cut into ¼-inch-wide strips
1 medium zucchini, cut crosswise into ¼-inch-thick slices
1 medium yellow squash, cut crosswise into ¼-inch-thick slices
3 tablespoons butter or margarine, melted
1 tablespoon chopped fresh thyme *or* 1 teaspoon dried thyme leaves
1 tablespoon chopped fresh basil *or* 1 teaspoon dried basil leaves
1 tablespoon chopped fresh chives or green onion tops
1 clove garlic, minced
¼ teaspoon salt
¼ teaspoon black pepper

1. Prepare grill for direct cooking.

2. Cut thin slice from base of mushroom stems with paring knife; discard. Thinly slice mushroom stems and caps. Combine mushrooms, bell pepper, zucchini and squash in large bowl. Combine butter, thyme, basil, chives, garlic, salt and black pepper in small bowl. Pour over vegetable mixture; toss to coat well.

3. Transfer mixture to 20×14-inch sheet of heavy-duty foil. Double fold top and ends of foil to seal packet. Place packet on grid. Grill, on covered grill, over medium coals 20 to 25 minutes or until vegetables are fork-tender. Open packet carefully to serve. *Makes 4 servings*

Nutrients per Serving (¼ of total recipe): 106 Calories, 5g Carbohydrate, 2g Dietary Fiber, 9g Total Fat, 6g Saturated Fat, 25mg Cholesterol, 247mg Sodium, 2g Protein

Herbed Mushroom Vegetable Medley

Szechuan-Grilled Mushrooms

1 pound large fresh mushrooms
2 tablespoons soy sauce
2 teaspoons peanut or vegetable oil
1 teaspoon dark sesame oil
1 clove garlic, minced
$\frac{1}{2}$ teaspoon crushed Szechuan peppercorns or red pepper flakes

1. Place mushrooms in large resealable plastic food storage bag. Add remaining ingredients to bag. Close bag securely; shake to coat mushrooms with marinade. Marinate at room temperature 15 minutes or cover and refrigerate up to 8 hours. (Mushrooms will absorb marinade.)

2. Thread mushrooms onto skewers. Grill or broil mushrooms 5 inches from heat 10 minutes or until lightly browned, turning once. Serve immediately.   *Makes 4 servings*

Variation: For Szechuan-Grilled Mushrooms and Onions, add 4 green onions, cut into $1\frac{1}{2}$-inch pieces, to marinade. Alternately thread onto skewers with mushrooms. Proceed as directed in step 2.

Nutrients per Serving ($\frac{1}{4}$ of total recipe): 61 Calories, 5g Carbohydrate, 2g Dietary Fiber, 4g Total Fat, 1g Saturated Fat, 0mg Cholesterol, 519mg Sodium, 4g Protein

Grilled Asparagus

1 pound fresh asparagus
    CRISCO® No-Stick Cooking Spray
$\frac{1}{2}$ teaspoon salt
$\frac{1}{4}$ teaspoon freshly ground black pepper

1. Prepare charcoal or gas grill. Trim woody stems off asparagus by breaking stalks. Spray asparagus with Crisco No-Stick Cooking Spray.

2. Grill asparagus for 3 minutes. Turn spears with tongs. Grill 3 to 4 minutes. Sprinkle with salt and pepper. Serve immediately.
Makes 4 servings

Nutrients per Serving ($\frac{1}{4}$ of total recipe): 14 Calories, 3g Carbohydrate, 1g Dietary Fiber, <1g Total Fat, <1g Saturated Fat, 0mg Cholesterol, 292mg Sodium, 1g Protein

Grilled Red Bell Pepper Dip

1 red bell pepper, stemmed, halved and seeded
1 cup ricotta cheese
4 ounces cream cheese
¼ cup (1 ounce) grated Parmesan cheese
  Grilled Garlic (recipe follows) *or* 1 clove garlic, minced
½ teaspoon Dijon mustard
¼ teaspoon salt
¼ teaspoon herbes de Provence*
  Fresh cut-up vegetables (optional)

*Substitute dash each rubbed sage, crushed dried rosemary, thyme, oregano, marjoram and basil leaves for herbes de Provence.

1. Grill bell pepper halves, skin side down, on covered grill over medium coals 15 to 25 minutes or until skin is charred, without turning. Remove from grill and immediately place in bowl; cover and let stand 15 to 20 minutes. Remove skin with paring knife; discard.

2. Place bell pepper in food processor. Add cheeses, garlic, mustard, salt and herbes de Provence; process until smooth. Serve with vegetables for dipping, if desired.   *Makes about 2 cups dip*

Grilled Garlic

2 cloves garlic
  Nonstick cooking spray

1. Soak wooden or bamboo skewer in water 20 minutes.

2. Thread garlic cloves onto skewer. Spray with cooking spray. Grill over medium coals about 8 minutes or until browned and tender. Or, place 2 garlic cloves on sheet of foil; lightly spray with cooking spray and carefully seal foil packet. Grill as directed.

Nutrients per Serving (¼ cup Dip (without vegetables)): 119 Calories, 3g Carbohydrate, <1g Dietary Fiber, 10g Total Fat, 6g Saturated Fat, 33mg Cholesterol, 187mg Sodium, 6g Protein

Grilled Baby Artichokes with Roasted Pepper Dip

18 baby artichokes* (about 1½ pounds)
½ teaspoon salt
¼ cup *Frank's® RedHot®* Original Cayenne Pepper Sauce
¼ cup butter or margarine, melted
   Roasted Pepper Dip (recipe follows)

1. Wash and trim tough outer leaves from artichokes. Cut ½-inch off top of artichokes, then cut in half lengthwise. Place artichoke halves, 1 cup water and salt in 3-quart microwavable bowl. Cover; microwave on HIGH 8 minutes or until just tender. Thread artichoke halves onto metal skewers.

2. Prepare grill. Combine *Frank's RedHot* Sauce and butter in small bowl. Brush mixture over artichokes. Place artichokes on grid. Grill, over hot coals, 5 minutes or until tender, turning and basting often with sauce mixture. Serve artichokes with Roasted Pepper Dip.   *Makes 6 servings*

Prep Time: 20 minutes
Cook Time: 13 minutes

Roasted Pepper Dip

1 jar (7 ounces) roasted red peppers, drained
1 clove garlic, chopped
¼ cup reduced-fat mayonnaise
2 tablespoons *French's®* Honey Dijon Mustard
2 tablespoons *Frank's® RedHot®* Original Cayenne Pepper Sauce
¼ teaspoon salt

1. Place roasted peppers and garlic in food processor or blender. Cover; process on high until very smooth.

2. Add mayonnaise, mustard, *Frank's RedHot* Sauce and salt. Process until well blended. Cover; refrigerate 30 minutes.   *Makes about 1 cup*

Prep Time: 10 minutes
Chill Time: 30 minutes

Nutrients per Serving (3 Artichokes plus 2 tablespoons Dip): 117 Calories, 9g Carbohydrate, 6g Dietary Fiber, 8g Total Fat, 4g Saturated Fat, 22mg Cholesterol, 370mg Sodium, 4g Protein

Grilled Baby Artichokes with Roasted Pepper Dip

Italian Grilled Vegetables

3 pounds assorted fresh vegetables*
1 cup CARB OPTIONS™ Italian Dressing

*Use any combination of the following, thickly sliced: eggplant, zucchini, yellow squash or large mushrooms.

1. In large, shallow nonaluminum baking dish or plastic bag, toss assorted fresh vegetables with Carb Options Italian Dressing. Cover, or close bag, and marinate in refrigerator, 15 minutes to 1 hour, turning once.

2. Remove vegetables from marinade, reserving marinade. Grill or broil vegetables, turning and basting occasionally with reserved marinade, until vegetables are tender.   *Makes 8 servings*

Preparation Time: 10 minutes
Marinate Time: 15 minutes
Cook Time: 15 minutes

Nutrients per Serving (⅛ of total recipe): 110 Calories, 8g Carbohydrate, 3g Dietary Fiber, 9g Total Fat, 2g Saturated Fat, 0mg Cholesterol, 370mg Sodium, 2g Protein

Grilled Summer Vegetables Alouette®

1 large aluminum foil cooking bag
3 cups fresh broccoli florets
3 cups sliced summer squash (any type)
2 medium red bell peppers, cut in strips
1 cup sliced mushrooms
1 (6.5-ounce) package *or* 2 (4-ounce) packages ALOUETTE®
   Garlic & Herbs

Preheat grill to medium high. Open foil bag, layer vegetables evenly inside, and spoon Alouette cheese on top. Seal bag by double-folding end. Place on grill and cook 8 to 10 minutes. Using oven mitts, carefully place bag on baking sheet and cut open, allowing steam to escape. If bag sticks to grill rack, cut open and remove vegetables (after grill cools, peel off bag). *Makes 6 servings*

Nutrients per Serving (1/6 of total recipe): 131 Calories, 9g Carbohydrate, 3g Dietary Fiber, 10g Total Fat, 6g Saturated Fat, 40mg Cholesterol, 199mg Sodium, 4g Protein

Hot Tip

A spray bottle filled with water is useful to control wild sparks and very small flare-ups on a charcoal grill. Care should be taken not to overuse the water spray and inadvertently extinguish the coals. Do not use water to quench flare-ups on a gas grill. Simply close the hood and turn down the heat until the flames subside.

ACKNOWLEDGMENTS

The publisher would like to thank the companies and organizations listed below for the use of their recipes and photographs in this publication.

Alouette® Cheese, Chavrie® Cheese, Saladena®

Butterball® Turkey

CanolaInfo.

The Kingsford Products Company

Lawry's® Foods

Mrs. Dash®

National Pork Board

North Dakota Beef Commission

Reckitt Benckiser Inc.

The J.M. Smucker Company

Unilever Bestfoods North America

Index

Artichokes: Grilled Baby Artichokes with Pepper Dip, 90
Asian Chicken Kabobs, 50
Asian Grilled Chicken, 44
Asian Grilled Steaks with Spicy Herb Sauce, 23
Asparagus
  Grilled Asparagus, 88
  Grilled Salmon Fillets, Asparagus and Onions, 78
August Moon Korean Ribs, 35
Avocado: Grilled Red Snapper with Avocado-Papaya Salsa, 66

Bacon: Seafood Kabobs, 76
Beef, Flank
  Marinated Grilled Steaks, 22
  Szechuan Grilled Flank Steak, 18
Beef, Ribeye: Peppered Beef Ribeye Roast, 20
Beef, Sirloin
  Grilled Beef Salad, 6
  Grilled Steak, 14
  Grilled Steak Italiano, 16
  Guadalajara Beef and Salsa, 10
  Herbed Beef Kabobs, 14
  Steak Provençal, 16
  Steaks with Creamy Mushroom Sauce, 17
Beef, Strip
  Asian Grilled Steaks with Spicy Herb Sauce, 23
  Honey Mustard Steaks with Grilled Onions, 9
  Peppercorn Steaks, 8
  Peppered Steak with Dijon Sauce, 4
  The Definitive Steak, 8
Bell Peppers
  Asian Chicken Kabobs, 50
  Glazed Pork and Pepper Kabobs, 34
  Grilled Red Bell Pepper Dip, 89
  Grilled Summer Vegetables Alouette®, 93
  Grilled Vegetables, 84
  Herbed Beef Kabobs, 14
  Herbed Mushroom Vegetable Medley, 86
  Marinated Italian Sausage and Peppers, 30
  Mixed Grill, 59
  Shrimp and Pineapple Kabobs, 64

South of the Border Turkey Kabobs, 53
Southwestern Kabobs, 29
Tex-Mex Pork Kabobs with Chili Sour Cream Sauce, 36
Broccoli: Grilled Summer Vegetables Alouette®, 93

Cajun Grilled Chicken, 52
Chicken, Breasts
  Asian Chicken Kabobs, 50
  Asian Grilled Chicken, 44
  Cajun Grilled Chicken, 52
  Grilled Chicken au Poivre Salad, 49
  Grilled Chicken with Chimichurri Salsa, 54
  Mustard Grilled Chicken with Dipping Sauce, 56
  Orange Vinaigrette Grilled Chicken Salad, 58
  Spicy Island Chicken, 48
  Thai Grilled Chicken, 57
Chicken, Tenders: Mixed Grill, 59
Chicken Tikka (Tandoori-Style Grilled Chicken), 46
Chicken, Whole
  Chicken Tikka (Tandoori-Style Grilled Chicken), 46
  Classic Grilled Chicken, 44
  Grilled Chicken, 58
  Rotisserie Chicken with Pesto Brush, 40
  Thai Barbecued Chicken, 42
Chili-Mustard Butter, 72
Classic Grilled Chicken, 44
Cuban Garlic & Lime Pork Chops, 24
Cucumber
  Cuban Garlic & Lime Pork Chops, 24
  Hot Shrimp with Cool Salsa, 62

Eggplant
  Grilled Vegetables, 84
  Mixed Grill, 59

Glazed Pork and Pepper Kabobs, 34
Grilled Asparagus, 88
Grilled Baby Artichokes with Pepper Dip, 90
Grilled Beef Salad, 6
Grilled Chicken, 58
Grilled Chicken au Poivre Salad, 49

Grilled Chicken with Chimichurri Salsa, 54
Grilled Chili-Marinated Pork, 26
Grilled Five-Spice Fish with Garlic Spinach, 70
Grilled Garlic, 89
Grilled Pork Tenderloin Medallions, 28
Grilled Pork Tenderloin with Apple Salsa, 38
Grilled Red Bell Pepper Dip, 89
Grilled Red Snapper with Avocado-Papaya Salsa, 66
Grilled Salmon Fillets, Asparagus and Onions, 78
Grilled Scallops and Vegetables with Cilantro Sauce, 74
Grilled Steak, 14
Grilled Steak Italiano, 16
Grilled Summer Vegetables Alouette®, 93
Grilled Swordfish á l'Orange, 82
Grilled Vegetables, 84
Guadalajara Beef and Salsa, 10

Herbed Beef Kabobs, 14
Herbed Mushroom Vegetable Medley, 86
Honey Mustard Steaks with Grilled Onions, 9
Horseradish-Mustard Spread, 30
Hot & Spicy Butter, 72
Hot Shrimp with Cool Salsa, 62

Italian Grilled Vegetables, 92

Jerk Ribs, 32

Kabobs & Skewers
  Asian Chicken Kabobs, 50
  Asian Grilled Chicken, 44
  Glazed Pork and Pepper Kabobs, 34
  Herbed Beef Kabobs, 14
  Mixed Grill, 59
  Seafood Kabobs, 76
  Shrimp and Pineapple Kabobs, 64
  South of the Border Turkey Kabobs, 53

Kabobs & Skewers *(continued)*
Southwestern Kabobs, 29
Tex-Mex Pork Kabobs with Chili Sour Cream Sauce, 36
Korean Beef Short Ribs, 12

Lobster: Lobster Tail with Tasty Butters, 72

Marinated Grilled Steaks, 22
Marinated Italian Sausage and Peppers, 30
Marinated Salmon with Lemon Tarragon Sauce, 68
Mesquite-Grilled Salmon Fillets, 80
Mixed Grill, 59
Mushrooms
Asian Chicken Kabobs, 50
Grilled Scallops and Vegetables with Cilantro Sauce, 74
Grilled Summer Vegetables Alouette®, 93
Herbed Beef Kabobs, 14
Herbed Mushroom Vegetable Medley, 86
Mixed Grill, 59
Steaks with Creamy Mushroom Sauce, 17
Szechuan-Grilled Mushrooms, 88
Mustard Grilled Chicken with Dipping Sauce, 56
Mustard-Grilled Red Snapper, 64

Orange Vinaigrette Grilled Chicken Salad, 58

Peppercorn Steaks, 8
Peppered Beef Ribeye Roast, 20
Peppered Steak with Dijon Sauce, 4
Pork, Chops
Cuban Garlic & Lime Pork Chops, 24
Pork Chops Italiano, 29
Southwestern Kabobs, 29
Pork, Loin: Glazed Pork and Pepper Kabobs, 34
Pork, Tenderloin
Grilled Chili-Marinated Pork, 26
Grilled Pork Tenderloin Medallions, 28

Grilled Pork Tenderloin with Apple Salsa, 38
Tex-Mex Pork Kabobs with Chili Sour Cream Sauce, 36

Red Snapper
Grilled Red Snapper with Avocado-Papaya Salsa, 66
Mustard-Grilled Red Snapper, 64
Ribs
August Moon Korean Ribs, 35
Jerk Ribs, 32
Korean Beef Short Ribs, 12
Roasted Pepper Dip, 90
Rotisserie Chicken with Pesto Brush, 40

Salads
Grilled Beef Salad, 6
Grilled Chicken au Poivre Salad, 49
Orange Vinaigrette Grilled Chicken Salad, 58
Salmon
Grilled Five-Spice Fish with Garlic Spinach, 70
Grilled Salmon Fillets, Asparagus and Onions, 78
Marinated Salmon with Lemon Tarragon Sauce, 68
Mesquite-Grilled Salmon Fillets, 80
Salsa, 10
Sausage
Marinated Italian Sausage and Peppers, 30
Mixed Grill, 59
Scallion Butter, 72
Scallops: Grilled Scallops and Vegetables with Cilantro Sauce, 74
Seafood Kabobs, 76
Shrimp
Hot Shrimp with Cool Salsa, 62
Seafood Kabobs, 76
Shrimp and Pineapple Kabobs, 64
Sour Cream
Marinated Salmon with Lemon Tarragon Sauce, 68
Sour Cream Sauce, 20
Tex-Mex Pork Kabobs with Chili Sour Cream Sauce, 36

South of the Border Turkey Kabobs, 53
Southwestern Kabobs, 29
Spiced Turkey with Fruit Salsa, 54
Spicy Island Chicken, 48
Spinach: Grilled Five-Spice Fish with Garlic Spinach, 70
Squash
Grilled Scallops and Vegetables with Cilantro Sauce, 74
Grilled Summer Vegetables Alouette®, 93
Herbed Mushroom Vegetable Medley, 86
South of the Border Turkey Kabobs, 53
Steak Provençal, 16
Steaks with Creamy Mushroom Sauce, 17
Swordfish
Grilled Swordfish á l'Orange, 82
Seafood Kabobs, 76
Szechuan Grilled Flank Steak, 18
Szechuan-Grilled Mushrooms, 88
Szechuan Tuna Steaks, 60

Tex-Mex Pork Kabobs with Chili Sour Cream Sauce, 36
Thai Barbecued Chicken, 42
Thai Grilled Chicken, 57
The Definitive Steak, 8
Tomatoes, Fresh
Grilled Beef Salad, 6
Grilled Chicken au Poivre Salad, 49
Mixed Grill, 59
Salsa, 10
Steak Provençal, 16
Tuna: Szechuan Tuna Steaks, 60
Turkey
South of the Border Turkey Kabobs, 53
Spiced Turkey with Fruit Salsa, 54
Turkey Teriyaki, 45

Zucchini
Asian Chicken Kabobs, 50
Grilled Scallops and Vegetables with Cilantro Sauce, 74
Grilled Vegetables, 84
Herbed Mushroom Vegetable Medley, 86